FIVE AMAZONIAN STUDIES

ON WORLD VIEW
AND CULTURAL CHANGE

INTERNATIONAL MUSEUM OF CULTURES

PUBLICATION 19

WILLIAM R. MERRIFIELD
Series Editor

DESMOND C. DERBYSHIRE
General Editor
Academic Publications Coordinator

FIVE AMAZONIAN STUDIES

ON WORLD VIEW
AND CULTURAL CHANGE

William R. Merrifield
editor

THE INTERNATIONAL MUSEUM OF CULTURES

Dallas, Texas

1985

Library of Congress Number: 85-080411

ISBN: 0-88312-174-3

ISSN: 0079-7669

This title is available at:

> THE INTERNATIONAL MUSEUM OF CULTURES
> 7500 W. Camp Wisdom Road
> Dallas, TX 75236

TABLE OF CONTENTS

PREFACE

This volume presents five studies from Amazonian communities of Brazil, Colombia, and Peru by field linguists of the Summer Institute of Linguistics. While each article has a focus of its own, their common thread is that of world view and cultural change.

At an ever-increasing rate, these communities are being impacted by modernizing influences from the outside. These articles document some of the results of this acculturative process as well as some of the underlying ideologies which provide the starting point for interpreting these influences by members of the communities.

In spite of much study, cultural change remains a little-understood phenomenon. Anthropologists do not yet have more than a very limited understanding of how or why cultures change. These studies are, therefore, welcome additions to the data base needed for the continuing pursuit of answers to these questions. The articles are presented in alphabetical order by language name: Candoshi (Peru), Guanano (Colombia), Karitiana (Brazil), Paumarí (Brazil), and Urubu-Kaapor (Brazil).

The first article, by Sheila Tuggy (of Scotland), challenges materialistic theories of change by outlining traditional values concerning violence of the fierce Jivaroan Candoshi-Shapra people of the northwestern Peruvian Amazon and by then showing how acceptance of a Candoshi version of the New Testament has amplified traditional views of God and of human relations. In particular, she suggests that the adoption of Christian ethical values finds support in traditional culture, Whitten (1981) notwithstanding, and implies other than the materialist motivations for attending to these influences imputed to the closely-related Ecuadorian Achuar by Taylor (1981).

1

The second study by Carolyn Waltz (of the USA)
details the traditional world view of the Tucanoan
Guanano of the Vaupés region of Colombia from the
point of view of a religious specialist (shaman) and
presents important insights into the difficult role
the traditional shaman plays in mediating the interac-
tion of human and nonhuman spirits. Although Waltz's
article does not focus upon change as such, she closes
her paper with suggestions regarding the viability of
this important role as traditionally practiced.

Moving to Brazil for the last three studies of
the volume, the first of these by Rachel Landin (of
England) presents a Lévi-Straussian analysis of four
Karitiana (Tupí) myths, examining the tensions implic-
it in the texts between unstructured and uncontrolla-
ble `nature´, on the one hand, and structured and
controlled `culture´, on the other. This is followed
by a brief introduction to problems of acculturation
being faced by the Arawakan Paumarí. Both the Karitiana and the Paumarí are undergoing extreme culture
stress, and Shirley Chapman (of England) focusses upon
economic aspects of Paumarí accommodation to a changing demography in the form of encroachment by the
Portuguese-speaking community of Brazil into their
traditional area. The study is preliminary and represents the situation as it was a decade ago, so that
another update on the current situation in the near
future would make a useful addition to it.

The volume closes with a comparative treatment of
the female puberty rites of a Tupí-Guaraní-speaking
community of Brazil, the Urubu-Kaapor. Kiyoko Kakumasu
(of the USA) compares these contemporary rites with a
sixteenth-century report of similar practices of the
Tupinambá which are taken to be a link to the pre-
cursors of present-day Urubu-Kaapor rites. Kakumasu
utilizes van Gennep's taxonomy of rites of passage as
a framework for her comparison and proposes that, in
spite of changes associated with a changing physical
and social environment, the rites continue to serve
the enculturative needs of the community as well as to
strengthen its ethnic identity against outside
influences.

One strength of these articles lies in the fact
that they come from the pens of women who have lived
among these five Amazonian peoples for many years.
They have learned to speak the local languages and

have come to know and respect--and have received the
respect of--the men, women, and children whose worlds
they here describe. The views they express about these
peoples are steeped in an intimate acquaintance with
the personal struggles of genuine friends and the
studies are presented to the larger community with an
attendant concern for their long-term well-being and
the attainment of their hopes and desires.

WILLIAM R. MERRIFIELD

Dallas, Texas
April, 1985

CANDOŚHI BEHAVIORAL CHANGE

Sheila C. Tuggy

Summer Institute of Linguistics, Peru

This article documents behavioral changes among the Candoshi of Northern Peru, as influenced by the introduction of the New Testament into the Candoshi language. The pursuit of power, prestige, and long life through supernatural means traditionally bound many Candoshi men to a life of violence. Frequently recognized as delusive, this power was nevertheless pursued to the point of near extermination of the society. Mistrust and fear thwarted two united peace-making attempts by Shuar and Candoshi war chiefs in the mid 1940's.

Since the translation of the New Testament into the Candoshi language, the people themselves have redirected their lives to obey their new perception of 'Father', the traditional Candoshi creator God. In so doing, they have eliminated a major proportion of the violence which formerly plagued them, while keeping other cultural values intact.

In the early 1920's the anthropologist Rafael Karsten wrote of the Shuar (Jivaro) people of Ecuador:

> The wars, the blood-feuds within the tribes, and the wars of extermination be-tween the different tribes are continuous, being nourished by their superstitious be-lief in witchcraft. These wars are the greatest curse of the Jivaros and are felt to be so even by themselves, at least so far as the feuds within the tribes are con-cerned. On the other hand, the wars are to such a degree one with their whole life and essence that only powerful pressure from

outside or a radical change of their whole
character and moral views could make them
abstain from them (Karsten 1923:1-2).

Today the Shuar and the neighboring Candoshi
peoples are living in relative peace. Their spirit
has not been broken by pressure from the outside world
but a deep behavioral change has taken place, the
foundation for which existed beforehand in traditional
Shuar and Candoshi spirit beliefs. This paper is a
review of traditional Candoshi values and spirit-world
beliefs and how they have been selectively reevaluated
by the Candoshi themselves in the light of the message
of the New Testament.

The paper proceeds by first sketching traditional
Candoshi values of good and evil, traditional beliefs
concerning the world, and the important concepts of
`protective powers´ outwardly expressed in acts of
violence. The following two sections then discuss the
nature of traditional warfare and the role of shamanism in Candoshi society. Finally, changes in these
traditional views and behaviors are described as they
were influenced by the introduction of the Candoshi
New Testament to the community over a period of thirty
years.

The heart of Candoshi territory lies to the north
and the west of Lake Rimachi in the northwestern
Peruvian Amazonia (Map 1). Information for this report
has been collected exclusively from Candoshi people of
the Chovinta and Chapori Rivers which flow into Lake
Rimachi from the North and West respectively, and from
Shapra people living on the Sicuanga and Pushaga
Rivers both of which are tributaries of the Morona
River. The Shapras and the Candoshi speak a language
which they all call `Candoshi´.[1] To facilitate the
writing of this paper the name Shapra will be used
only in referring exclusively to the Shapra people.

Members of the Summer Institute of Linguistics
(SIL), Loretta Anderson and Doris Cox, began work
among the Shapra people in 1950. Later Mary Beth
Hinson joined them. When Doris Cox was not able to
return to Peru, my husband, John, and I joined Lorrie
and Beth in 1959. Over the years other responsibilities have taken us away from the Candoshi for consid-
erable periods of time. Between the years 1959 and
1975, however, we spent a total of five years of

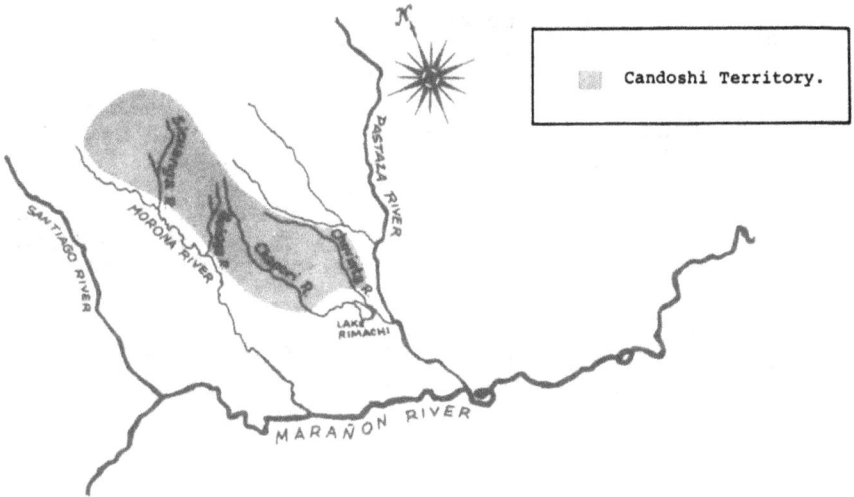

Map 1: Northwestern Peruvian Amazonia

actual living time in Candoshi communities.   Although
our primary responsibilities and interests centered
around linguistics and Bible translation, we have been
very aware of our need to understand the Candoshi
world view. John recorded the material for the book
Tariri, My Story (Wallis 1965). Beth Hinson and I
produced two short books of Candoshi folklore, diglot-
ted in Spanish for the bilingual schools.   Together
with the Candoshi I have recently compiled a book of
texts on Candoshi social activities and rituals which
we also hope to have published for the bilingual
schools in diglot form.

TRADITIONAL VALUES

     Contrary to the opinion of Professor Whitten
(1981:151), Christian premises set forth in the New
Testament can accord with indigenous thought. Individuality of the adult male and loyalty to family are the
two highest values of Candoshi society.   Each man
respects the individuality and independence of the
other.   A man does what he wants to do and no one
interferes with his decision or criticizes him.   This
foundation upon which the society stands allows a high
degree of behavioral variety within the Candoshi view
of good and evil.

     In spite of a traditional Candoshi preoccupation
with violence and death, killing was not considered
`good´ (vanasiri). This word is used of anything that
looks pretty, is well made, is not rotten or broken,
as well as for such values as kindness, happiness,
truthfulness, and honesty. Tanchima´s uncle, we were
told, had a `good heart´. When he came to visit, the
children were not sent, for safety, to the house of an
aunt, because uncle´s visits always made everyone
happy.   He did not get drunk and fight, but told
stories, played with the children, and made everyone
laugh. He had a good heart. He died in 1951.

     Old Santiago also had a good heart.   He never
went on war raids and, although he had only one son,
he did not insist that his wife strangle any one of
their five daughters at birth.   He loved them all and
took care of them.   Santiago was an old man when we
first met him in 1964. He died in 1967. The lives of
both of these men were, at the time, an unusual but
acceptable Candoshi life-style.

Acts considered bad (yotarita) include violent behavior in general, incest, adultery, premarital sexual relations, hate and its manifestations, anger, and stealing. Extramarital sexual relations, if publicized, are subject to the death penalty.

The word `ugly´ (mantsiri), is commonly used not just of appearance but of character. A man who had speared the bodies of women and children and thrown them into the river was described as ugly. A woman, after telling me of the violent and sexually lustful life of her father, summed up his character by saying, "My father was ugly." One group says of others who continually drink and brawl, "They live ugly."

It is difficult to evaluate accurately the Candoshi view of violence. Opinions differ depending on whether a person is on the giving or the receiving end. Killing is bad (yotarita) because it causes so much suffering, not only to the victims who are often wounded and then tortured to death, but also to the widows and orphans.

On the other hand, it was `right´ (varitariya) to avenge a death. To some men, especially those who had pursued spirit powers, killing was a thrill, a diversion which they looked forward to from one raid to the next.

THE TRADITIONAL CANDOSHI WORLD

The Candoshi world consists of two realms: the lower world of forest, rivers, mountains and whatever may lie beyond (tsaporonasi), and the upper world above the earth (kaninta). The entrance to the upper world is continually opening and closing like gigantic scissors which keeps it almost isolated from the world below. The hummingbird, because of his expertise in hovering and darting, has contact with the upper world; but no one knows what he sees there. Our Father (apanchi) has his home in the upper world. The lower world is inhabited by humans (tpotsi), spirits of the dead (tsipari vani), evil spirits (yashinko), phantom spirits (kanizi), rainbow people (tsonki tpotsi), and all other faunal and floral life. Traditional Candoshi beliefs concerning Our Father and the general kinds of beings which inhabit the lower world are sketched in the following sections.

Our Father

Candoshi mythological history can be divided into two eras--that in which Father frequently appeared in the lower world, and the present era in which he still has an interest in helping people but no longer appears in visible form. The following mythological incident precipitated a transition between the first and second eras:

> Father's son came down to the world to enjoy life with people. On the whole the adults treated him well, but the children were jealous of his abilities in hunting and fishing. One day the children threw sand in his eyes and, although a man came along to help the crying child clean out his eyes, his father was still very angry. He sent a storm of wind and rain on the earth causing a flood which destroyed all the people, with the exception of the man who had been kind to the child....When the water had receded, the man took a parrot as his wife. She became a woman and bore children from all parts of her body at one time. These children she later sent away, in different directions. They became the founders of the different nations of the world.

The details of this story (here omitted) vary from one individual to another, but the basic facts are stable. Following this incident Father never appeared to people again.

During the first era Father made the world, people, and all fauna and flora. At first he made people with hard flesh. In those days people lived until they were so old that they had to crawl around, but still could not die. Eventually Father said, "People suffer too much living such a long life," and he made people with soft flesh. Now people die at a much younger age.

Father instructed people in the art of living. He taught them how to plant gardens so that the produce was ready to harvest in a few days. He taught men how they could cause a tree to split and fall in the form of two canoes. Later, a man seeing this for the first time, called out in fright as the canoes fell, and since that time man has had to work hard to make canoes.

Father was opposed to violence. He turned a family of warriors into a herd of wild boar because of the suffering they were causing others. A particular story records how Father had pity on those rejected by society. Two women who had been tricked into cohabiting with a strong-smelling man named Camphor were thereby made repulsive to all other men. Father turned these women into the annatto tree and the genipa tree. Then all the male birds habitually cohabiting with the women took on the deeper colors of the red annatto and the black genipa.

During the present mythological era, although Father does not appear in visible form, he still has an interest in the well-being of people in providing their physical needs. Plants still grow in the gardens, although more slowly, and there are still fish in the rivers and game in the forest. Father provides medicinal plants to treat sicknesses. When life is happy--when there is plenty of food (especially wild meat), when people recover from illness, when potential dangers are averted--the Candoshi say, "Father is helping us" (Apap istakiya). But when life is hard, they very often say, "Father is punishing us (Apap vaniakiya) because we have been living wrongly."

Father is so much a part of Candoshi folklore that very often his appearance on the scene is marked only by the word kushon `at this point Father intervened´. This is always the turning point of a story, the beginning of the resolution.

Father was traditionally neither worshipped nor appeased, he was simply accepted as a force in everyday life. In contrast to Father, the spirits who inhabit the earth are either harmless or malevolent.

Spirits of the dead

Spirits of the dead (tsipari vani) wander in the forest until they tire of wandering, at which time they probably disappear; but no one really knows. They are pitied more than feared. Occasionally one becomes visible as a phantom (kanizi).

A Shapra woman of the Pushaga River tells how her husband had seen the phantom spirit of an old man sitting on a log by the edge of the river. He recognized the phantom as a man who had died a few years previously. The woman's husband stood still and watched it until it finally vanished.

Spirits of the dead enter into birds or animals in order to communicate with the living, forewarning of impending misfortune. The following examples are from a text written by Yampisa Shotka of the Pushaga River in February, 1983.

> When a person walking in the forest hears a tiger sounding, "Mm mm," the people say that the spirit of a dead person has made himself into a tiger to speak to someone. Therefore, when a man hears that sound he goes and looks for the tiger's footprints. When he sees that the tiger has been following him he says to himself, "How is it that that tiger is predicting evil towards me even though I am a powerful man?"

> A certain small bird (tinka) also warns us. If someone hears a tinka sing close by, "Tin tin tin, tin tin tin," he knows that a close relative is going to die. If he hears it sing far away, he knows that a distant relative will die.

> Spirits also turn themselves into the metori bird. If the metori sings, "Chiikó," just as a man is making plans to do something, the man will be afraid and say, "Chaa! I had better not do that." But if, when he is planning, the metori says, "Tsi tsits," that is a good sign and he will go ahead with his plans. We trust a lot in these omens from the spirits.

Spirits of the dead also appear to the living as phantom animals or birds when they want to pass on spirit-power (arotama) to them.

Evil spirits

Evil spirits (yashinko) oppose the well-being of man. To see an evil spirit in phantom form always results in death. A man attacked by an evil spirit immediately goes insane and rushes into the forest where he usually kills himself. If he is rescued and suppressed by relatives, his violent behavior eventually gives way to a chronic psychotic state of alternating irrationality and deep depression.

Paradoxically it is evil spirits which give a man the basic spirit power (arotama) which makes him a strong persuasive orator and preserves his life from death by violence; but, as with the Shuar (Harner 1972:112), it is also this same spirit power which goads him to violence and warfare.

Phantoms

In its generic sense, the word kanizi means 'phantom', either in human or animal form. Kanizi is the word most commonly heard in reference to the spirit world and probably one of the words most quickly learned with overtones of fear by the Candoshi child. The Candoshi say of tinka or metori birds that they are phantoms. The ancestral spirit sitting on the log was a phantom. Apparitions of rainbow people are phantoms. But the most fearful of all apparitions are the phantoms seen from time to time in the forest, usually beautifying themselves--braiding their hair or painting their faces with annatto dye. These are evil spirits (yashinko). The following is an excerpt from a text by Visho of Huambracocha recorded in the 1960's:

> There is a different kind of sickness that infects people who see a phantom. We do not know where phantoms live, but perhaps they live in the trees. Once in a while they come out to comb their hair and paint their faces, or perhaps just to go for a walk. If a child should so much as catch a glimpse of a phantom, the phantom will lock up the child's spirit in its home. When this happens it is definitely an evil spirit (yashinko).

> The child vomits and vomits. He has a high fever and rapidly becomes exhausted. I saw my brother's child like that. He vomited repeatedly and had diarrhea that was black. When a child is like that there is no hope

for him and he dies. We call that the
phantom-seeing disease. We do not even try
tobacco because they always die. "He has
been bewitched by having seen a phantom," we
say.

Unseen phantoms control thunder, earthquakes, and
the sudden violent winds and rain storms which blow up
unexpectedly in the western Marañón area. The occurrence of any of these phenomena is greatly feared. If
a phantom of the elements grabs a person's soul as it
goes by, the person dies within a few days. A soul
grabbed in this way will never be free to wander in
the forest but will be continually driven by the
phantom of the elements.

Rainbow people

Rainbow people (tsonki tpotsi) live in the rivers
and are seen from time to time along riverbanks,
usually by someone drifting slowly and quietly downstream. Although not aggressively harmful to man, the
rainbow people do grab anyone who accidentally encoun-
ters them on the riverbank and drag them down into the
water. The Candoshi say that shards of ancient pottery
found throughout the area were made by rainbow people
and warn their children not to touch them lest the
rainbow people harm them.

PROTECTIVE POWERS

The Candoshi traditionally practiced ritual can-
nibalism of enemy war victims. Oral tradition indicates that, at some time in the past, two Candoshi men
spent time among the neighboring Achuar being instructed in the pursuit of spirit power (Candoshi:
arotama; Shuar: arotum) and learning the art of head
shrinking and sorcery (Wallis 1965:37-38). The two
ancestors spent only a short time among the Achuar.
They had not taken their wives with them and suffered
lack of food and sexual relations. They did, however,
learn the basic facts of all three subjects, which
they then contextualized in terms of their own world
view. It is possible, but far from certain, that
until this time Candoshi shamans practiced only heal-
ing ceremonies.

Among the Candoshi, peripheral beliefs about obtaining spirit power vary from one person to another; but central beliefs are stable, namely, a man must sleep in the forest for several nights, he must observe a strict fast, he must drink tobacco juice, a phantom must appear to him, he must ask for power, and the phantom gives him power.

Spirit power

Basic spirit power (arotama) which a man needs for preservation of life and which makes him a fearless killer comes from an evil spirit (yashinko). A young man seeks this power whenever he himself wants it, usually in his middle or later teen years. He does not advertise the fact that he is going to the forest to have a vision and, even if his quest is successful, he mentions it to no one except perhaps to his wife. The people soon see a change in his character and his strong desire to kill. Almost invariably he organizes a war raid in which his relatives are obligated to support him.

The following is an excerpt from a text by Masho Kamarampi of the Chapori River, recorded in 1970.

I will tell you how people have visions of spirit power. This is what a man does in order to have a vision: He sleeps out in the forest and does not eat. He does not even drink one drop of cassava beer. When he gets to a point of desperation from hunger and thirst, he drinks tobacco juice until he is intoxicated. Then he calls out to the spirit power, "Arotama, help me to kill people and to live forever." That is what he always says.

A phantom of an evil spirit (yashinko kanizi) hears him calling for spirit power and says to himself, "It sounds like he really wants me." So when the man loses consciousness, the evil spirit appears to him and says, "This is what I kill people with. I kill them without even touching them," and he produces a glistening ball, hard like stone, and puts it in the man's mouth [which he swallows]. Then, so that the

man will aim accurately when he fires his
gun, the evil spirit puts another shining
stone in his hand.

The man then wakes up. He says,
"Hmmmm." He feels his heart pounding and he
says, "I have had a vision. Cha cha cha cha
cha! What is its purpose?" He always says
that. Then he rolls up his mosquito net, and
although it is still night he goes home.

Later in the morning, having bathed and
painted his face with annatto, having tied
up his hair and put on his crown of toucan
feathers, the man goes from house to house
inviting all his relatives and friends to
come to his house. Then he returns home and
continues to drink the strongly fermented
liquid which collects at the bottom of the
cassava beer jar.

Then taking his drum he beats it in
rhythm. Tin tin tin tin! Making his wife
stand up he says to her, "If it is time for
me to die, I will probably die and you will
have to live alone. We men tend to get
killed. Father made me a man; he made you a
woman." This he wails to his wife [beating
his drum].

His wife is very sad to hear this. "My
husband will probably die. He must have had
a very bad vision that makes him want to
kill people," she says. She is very sad.

The man keeps on wailing and singing,
all the time talking of death, because the
evil spirit, the spirit power has entered
him. Because of this he talks continually of
death.

Suddenly he grabs his gun and starts
shooting at the trees. Then he says, "That
is how I will shoot when I am far away."
Although he is shooting at the trees, he is
talking about people. He keeps on shooting
and shooting until his wife says to him,
"Don't finish off all your shells. You are a
man. You have to shoot meat for your fami-

ly." He stops shooting and says, "You are right, but I feel a burning anger, just like you women feel when you get angry. The vision that I had is making me enraged."

But for him that is good as he has to persuade the people to kill.

The text then goes on to tell of the arranging and carrying out of the war raid (see below).

There are additional powers which a Candoshi man can acquire from ancestral spirits disguised as animals or birds. Although these powers also promise long life and power, each one also has an additional benefit to offer.

Tiger power

Tiger power makes a person a fearless killer. A man who has tiger power is afraid of nothing. Even real tigers slink away from him if he speaks to them strongly. The following excerpt is from a text by Tariri Nochamata, River Pushaga, 1965:

I saw a tiger playing with her cub. As they played they pounced around together. "Why are they doing that?" I thought. They were not afraid of me. The mother stood there and licked her cub all over. I was fishing [in a canoe] and they did not notice me at first. Then she saw me, but she just looked and kept on licking the head of her cub. I thought, "How come they are not afraid of me? I am close enough to shoot them. Maybe they are spirit power," I said. That is what we Shapra always say when we see an animal behaving strangely. "Perhaps it is spirit power," we say. "Perhaps it is behaving like that because it wants to talk to me," we say...." You must be a phantom and want to speak to me. Speak to me. Speak to me," I said. As I spoke I stood up in the canoe with a harpoon in my hand. That scared them and they ran off into the forest.

That night I did not sleep at home. I said to Irina, "Sleep by yourself with the

children. I am going to look for the tiger
in the forest." I went and I waited a long
time. How many nights did I wait? I do not
know. I was sleeping under my mosquito net
when I awoke suddenly. I heard the tiger
coming. It walked around and around the net.
My heart was pounding. I was scared to move.
Then I said, "If you are the spirit of
Chiriapa or some other ancestor, give me
your power." The tiger stopped. I could feel
its breath on my face. It breathed hard on
me. Then it went away. That is how I got the
tiger power. That is all.

Anaconda power

Anaconda power keeps a man from fear in warfare
and gives him flesh like the anaconda that does not
readily bleed. The following text was recorded by
Visho of Huambracocha, in 1964:

There are many kinds of spirit power.
It enters into many different things to give
us power. The anaconda also gives us power.
A man may be walking through the forest, or perhaps traveling on the river, and
suddenly see an anaconda lying there curled
up asleep. If he later sees this same thing
in a dream then he will probably say, "I am
going to wait for it. I am going to wait
right by where it is asleep. It must be a
phantom that is saying, 'Come and see me.'
That must be why it is just lying there."

He goes to where the anaconda is lying
and he pokes it with a long stick or with
his paddle and says, "Speak to me." Then he
sleeps right there.

When he is sleeping a phantom man comes
running towards him from the anaconda and he
says, "Why are you not afraid even of that
anaconda? Why is it that although I have a
heart just like yours, I am afraid? My heart
is just like yours," he says.

The man replies, "Yes, you are right.
You are just a man like me. Give me your

power." Then the phantom man says, "I am also a man," and he shoots his power into the man. "Now you have a heart just like mine. I can see it in your eyes. Now you will be able to kill people with this, without even touching them," he says, and he gives the man a red thing like a small stone. "Open your mouth," he says, and when the man opens his mouth the phantom puts the stone in it. If the man cannot swallow that one he gives him another one that is slippery. "Open your mouth," he says, and the slippery one slips down easily.

Then the man hears a voice coming from inside him, "When you have killed just one person you will go on living. You will not die." Then the man says, "That is it. I have it. I will live forever. I will not die."

That is what they say, and they now belong to the evil spirit (yashinko). Even though the man never dreams again of the anaconda, even when he is very very old, he keeps on living.

Old Kashkona once said to us boys, "Boys, when you see the anaconda, just tell me and I will help you. You have to tie up his head with a vine and make a cage around him. I will help you. We will stay there and sleep and if you do that without eating or drinking, the anaconda will certainly give you his power." That is what Kashkona said.

Although we boys saw anaconda from time to time, we never told Kashkona. We said, "Who is he kidding! Who wants to tie up the head of an anaconda?" We were really scared, so we said nothing to Kashkona. Those who do have the anaconda power, however, really know how to kill people. If they are shot they do not bleed so they do not die. Only a liquid-like serum comes from the wound. That is why they do not die. That is all.

The problem remained that experience belied belief. Many people were killed, all of whom claimed to have spirit power. Maxkina Shotka, of the Sicuanga

River, recently told me of his uncle, who came to their home one day boasting that he had received spirit power from the Condor. Condor power is considered to be the ultimate of all powers which give protection. After a few days Maxkina's uncle went around from house to house arranging a war party which he himself was going to lead. His power would be strong enough to guarantee safety for all involved. Not all believed that he had received the Condor power, but Maxkina and a number of others went along on the raid. When the fighting began his uncle was the first of their party to be killed.

Attempts are made to rationalize the contradictory evidence, the most common being, "He thought he had the power but was mistaken," or "His power was weak that day." People, however, did seriously question the efficacy of it. Tariri Nochamata once said, "I knew that the only way I could be safe was to keep on killing so that people would be afraid of me and afraid to attack me." Maxkina Shotka stated that, following the experience of his uncle, he came to the conclusion that all so-called spirit power was probably a delusion.

The theory of waxing and waning power, which seems to be well developed among the Shuar (Harner 1972:140-41), is vague in Candoshi thought. The Candoshi believe that the more a man kills the stronger he becomes. They never seem to feel the need of seeking new basic power. Rather they seek additional ancestral power through the encouragement of having seen phantom animals.

WARFARE AND KILLING

Organized raids are carried out by a group of from twenty to thirty men against an enemy of one of the group or against a group whose existence is a threat to the attackers. The Candoshi have historically preserved their isolation by annihilating neighboring groups. Their reason was interestingly expressed in the following words:

Our people just wanted to live in peace. So whenever a group threatened us, either because they were living too close to our territory or because of their aggressive behavior, we just killed them.

Most war raids, however, were for the purpose of revenge. All killings, whether by witchcraft or violence, had to be revenged. Prior to the introduction of firearms, battles were fought with spears at close range with equal danger to both sides. Firearms gave a much greater advantage to the attackers who could shoot from the protection of trees. By the mid 1940's war raids had reached an unprecedented level (Taylor 1981:651, Descola 1981:625).

Apart from war raids, the killing of individuals, usually as punishment for a social offense, was also common practice. Anyone caught in the act of illicit sexual intercourse, either by a woman's husband or by an unmarried girl's father or brother, could only expect death. Both the man and the woman were killed. No doubt some fathers did not kill their daughters, but in general this was the law. If a widow or an unmarried woman became pregnant, the man responsible for her was expected to kill her, and usually did.

Killings were not uncommon when groups were visiting and drinking together. Suspicion always ran high even between neighboring groups. If someone in the party were visiting from a far-away group, the probability of him being a spy made him even more suspect. Only a ritual friendship system, in which two unrelated men from different areas take an oath of mutual respect and trust, makes it possible for an individual to journey far from home. Even a ritual friend, however, has been known to betray his friend when his own life was threatened by a restless community looking for someone to kill.

Young men occasionally show off their power prowess by killing an orphaned sister. We are aware of two cases in which teen-age boys attempted to strangle their sisters, but the girls were rescued, the first one by SIL colleagues and the second by a Christian relative. In the first case, the excuse was given that he did not want to be responsible for her, and in the second, that she had been living promiscuously.

It is impossible to state, with any degree of certainty, how many Candoshi men abstained from killing altogether and how many only went along on raids when obligated to do so. At a rough estimate perhaps 5% would not kill at all and as many as 40% avoided killing as much as possible. These latter were not of a violent temperament.

The following text by Masho Kamarampi is a continuation of the text on spirit power excerpted above. Here he describes the organizing and carrying out of the war raid. The war challenge and other prewar rituals are not mentioned in the text, nor were enemy heads taken. Other Candoshi agree, however, that this is a good general account of a raid.

> The people who had been invited arrived at the house. The man's wife told the women who had come with their husbands, "My husband must have had a bad vision to kill people. He's talking bad [of killing] and drinking a lot of cassava beer, but not getting drunk."

> The women say, "Are you sure?"

> She replies, "Yes, I am sure. Look how my husband is drinking," she says.

> The women on hearing this tell their respective husbands, "She says that he has had a vision and he wants to go kill."

> The husbands say, "Yes, she is probably right. Our brother has probably had a vision," and they all put their confidence in that, even the old men.

> They decide that they want to go and kill and they enlist others to join them. When a good number of people have agreed to go, twenty-five or thirty people, then they get organized. There are always two war chiefs who go along, and under them are others experienced in war who are like sergeants. Then there are the rest of us, the soldiers, who also know a little bit about war. The two chiefs tell the sergeants what they want to have done and the sergeants tell us soldiers.

If everyone agrees, the chiefs are really happy. Then we all set out on the trail. Those who really do not want to go suffer from fear throughout the journey. The chiefs say to the soldiers, "We will do what we said back at the house. We will not get drunk, because if we do we will probably not talk sensibly. If we stay sober we will plan well," they say. The sergeants tell the soldiers and the soldiers say, "Yes, that is good, because men always die in raids."

The chiefs are happy when they hear that the men are in agreement. Having eaten, they send out spies to look over the situation.

When the whole party arrives near the enemy homes, they get together on the trail, and someone says, "Well, what will we do?" Others say, "We will do what we said we would do." By this time those who do not want to kill are trembling with fear and one will say, "I will take care of the canoes." The chief will say, "Okay, you take care of the canoes." That is good because we always need someone to take care of the canoes.

Then the rest go ahead and surround the houses. The two chiefs talk together and say, "What will we do?" They decide to shoot the main enemy together so that there will not be much chance of missing him. When they see him they both shoot. Then all the soldiers say, "Now he is dead. There is nothing to be afraid of. We can all kill now." They shoot until all the men have been killed. They leave the dead lying face down on the ground. They do not go and turn them over, they leave them face down.

Then they say, "Let's go. Now that they are all dead perhaps they will live happily."

That is what they always say, but it is a stupid thing to say because they were living happily until the enemy came along and killed them. But that is what they always say. Being dead they cannot hear them say it, but maybe their spirits hear.

Then they all go home to their wives and their cassava beer. When they get home they fast for a few days and eat only mota [a tuber of the Araceae family].

SHAMANISM

Shamanism is also a major cause of Candoshi warfare. Deaths attributed to bewitching shamanism must be revenged.

Shaman power is used either to cure or to kill. In either case, power is transmitted to the patient or victim through a spirit anaconda. The struggle is, thus, between a bewitching shaman who sends the anaconda to capture the spirit of his victim and a curing shaman who attempts to manipulate the anaconda to release the spirit of his patient.

Shaman power is passed on from a shaman to an apprentice shaman through a series of ritual ceremonies and the ever-increasing observance of taboos. Most Candoshi men practice curing shamanism to some extent or other. Only when home treatment has failed does a family resort to paying a more renowned shaman.

There are very few Candoshi bewitching shamans. The restrictions involved in first obtaining this power and then in keeping it are extremely inhibiting, and bewitching shamans are too often the victims of revenge killings. Candoshi prefer to seek the services of an Achuar shaman when such services are required.

To the Candoshi, sickness falls into four categories. There is often doubt regarding the category to which an illness belongs, and the failure of one treatment will cast the diagnosis into another category. The four categories are as follows:

1. Anaconda entering (isariya pshtokiya)

A spirit anaconda steals the spirit of a person and puts his own spirit in the human body. Symptoms of this include all subacute and chronic intestinal infections and infestations. They are cured by shaman power and the use of tobacco smoke or tobacco juice.

The following text by Visho of Huambracocha explains the practice of the curing shaman and some of the theory behind shamanism in general.

The anaconda takes away a child's spirit and the child is left without a spirit. It is the anaconda that takes spirits. He takes them down to his dark home, shoves them inside, and locks them in. What is his home like? What kind of a place is it? How can a person really know?....

Having locked a child's spirit up in his dark place, how can the child possibly eat well? He just lives without any energy or desire to eat. His parents say, "Our child is probably going to die. The anaconda has taken his spirit and locked it up in his home. How can the child possibly live?"

[They go to a shaman.]

"Will you blow [tobacco smoke] for us? I will bring my child and show him to you and we will pay you for blowing," they say....

[The shaman agrees and proceeds with several hours of preparation.]

The shaman breathes smoke all over the child's body. Then warning the mother not to let the child grab the cigar, he bends the child's head forward and blows smoke into his nostrils and his mouth. That is the end of the treatment.

The following day, or after one night's sleep, the child's fever goes down and he is better. If it happens like that then everybody knows that he had really been bewitched by the anaconda. That is what the old Candoshi have always said.

2. Dart shot (mpappat shogtariya)

A second category of illness results from a shaman having caused bewitching darts to enter a person's
body with intent to kill. The more powerful shamans
can do this just by looking at a person, but Candoshi
shamans usually send the darts through the intermedi-
ary spirit anaconda. Symptoms are usually in the nature of a sudden acute illness with high fever, severe
headache, and attacks of vertigo. Abscesses, boils,
and other debilitating skin infections also come into
this category, as do sudden deaths from any cause,
especially convulsions, hemorrhage, or any fatal
accident.

Only another bewitching shaman can cure these
illnesses. He must first find out who has been responsible for the bewitching by drinking ayahuasca, an
hallucinogenic drug made from the vine Banisteriopsis.
This enables him to see a vision of the culprit. He
then attempts to remove the darts and, by manipulation
of the spirit anaconda sends them, via the anaconda,
back to that person. If the person does not die within
a short period, a more direct attempt is made to kill
him. Visho continues his discussion of shamanism as
follows:

A shaman sends the anaconda. "Go and do
this," he says, and sends the anaconda with
his infecting power. How is it done? Perhaps
the power sticks to the anaconda. When the
shaman commands him, the anaconda goes and
shoots darts into the person but it is under
the orders of a person. Shamans do this.
They command the anaconda and he goes and
shoots darts into a person.

There are some shamans, however, who
can shoot darts just by talking. When a
shaman does this, the person hears him and
knows, so he goes to another shaman who also
knows about darts and this shaman says,
"Aha! This infection is not from the anaconda, it is from a person." Then he drinks
ayahuasca. When he is intoxicated he says,
"Yes, that is who it is. That is the one who
sent the anaconda." Then he pulls out the
darts....

What is it they say? I was at an Achuar
community and the shaman was saying, "Awi wi
wi wi wi!" I was sitting in a canoe down on
the river below the bank and someone said,
"That is the shaman curing someone who has
been infected by the anaconda." I had come
alone bringing a mestizo to the shaman. The
people were all gathered in his house, but I
stayed alone in the canoe. The Achuar shaman
was beating his drum, shaking branches of
the shogoshogo bush, and stamping his feet
in rhythm. I was really scared.

Suddenly the shaman came to the edge of
the bank and shouted to me, "Come on up."
But I said to myself, "Not on your life.
When a shaman is drugged like that he shoots
darts into you." I took off downstream in
the canoe. Anyone would be scared of them
the way they are all painted up and drugged.
They say to you, "Who do you think you are?
Do you think that you are a shaman too?" and
then they shoot darts into you. Just looking at you with their eyes they shoot darts
into your body.

3. Phantom seeing (kanizi pamarini)
and demon possession (yashinko pshtokiya)

These are both described above. There is no
treatment.

4. White man's diseases (kiristiyan tsotamarini)

These include all epidemic infections and tuber-
culosis, and are treated with white man's medicines.
They are often thought of also as darts shot by a
white man.

FATHER'S WORD AS CHANGE AGENT

Although good and evil were well defined by the
Candoshi, for the greater majority of men there was no
compulsion to focus on the `good' aspects of life
which would have promoted general peace and construc-
tive interpersonal relationships. The Candoshi creator

Our Father had let it be known in the past that he desired peace and happiness for his `children`, but the human drive for self-preservation even at the expense of the lives of others was by far the more urgent consideration. Spirit power, which promised life preservation, goaded men to kill. Having killed they lived in constant fear of revenge. Fear of revenge generated more killing.

The message of the New Testament was introduced gradually to the Candoshi as it was translated into their language. From the beginning, the people identified the God of the Bible as Our Father (Apanchi). The Bible did not contradict the traditional Candoshi view of God but rather expanded it. That Father's son had come to the world to give his life as a propitiatory sacrifice for the evil of mankind, that he was resurrected from death and now offered eternal life to those who would accept his sacrifice was a significant change from the traditional story of Father's son. Father did not just vaguely desire that his creation live in peace with a spirit of brotherly love; at great personal cost he had provided a means whereby mankind could be free from the power of evil and live in peace. The miraculous healings of the Gospels greatly expanded the Candoshi concept of Father as a God of positive love. Both Father and Father's son were intimately concerned with suffering humanity.

Gradually Father was brought from the periphery of Candoshi awareness to the very center of the struggle for life. The issue now became a choice between following the way of Father or the way of the evil spirits. As in all of Candoshi life, each man decided for himself which course he would take, his wife and children usually following his decision.

A wedge in the cycle of warfare

In 1954, Tariri Nochamata, a Shapra war chief living on the Pushaga river, became a Christian with a surprising compulsion to obey Father's Words. In 1955, the family of Shotka, also living on the Pushaga River, attacked Tariri's family, killing his wife's brother and seriously wounding Tariri. When he recovered from his injuries, he withstood all pressure to take revenge.

Shotka and his family left the Pushaga and settled on the Sicuanga River where most of his descendents are now living. Within a year Tsovinki, one of Shotka's group, and a young companion were captured by Tariri and his men on the Morona River. Tariri did not kill them. He said, "Father says that we should love our enemies and treat them kindly." He kept Tsovinki a prisoner for almost three months, told him the little he knew of Father's Word, and then let him go home. Speaking of the events of 1955 Tariri later said:

> When I stopped killing people did not fear me any more. They came to kill me. They were very close to me when they shot me. I do not know how I escaped death. Father did not want me to die. He wanted me to know something of the suffering which I had caused other people.

> My people still do not understand why I will not go out and take revenge. Before, I was always leading raids for other people; but now, when I should be revenging my own injury and my brother-in-law's death, I am at peace.

The refusal of a leading war chief to revenge an attempt on his life proved to be the wedge which broke the apparently unbreakable cycle of Candoshi warfare. From this time on, the Shapras on the Pushaga River stopped killing. Shotka's group on the Sicuanga River remained aggressively violent until 1967 when several of their number became Christians.

During the late 1950's and early 1960's a number of Candoshi on the Chapori River also became Christians. Christian people were no longer a threat to their former enemies, which lessened the number of potential antagonists and gradually reduced the incessant pressure to keep on killing. When those holding to the traditional life-style did try to organize a war raid, fewer men were available to participate. More and more they found themselves making temporary alliances with unrelated men in order to attack an enemy group. They acknowledged Father's way as a legitimate way of life and, unwittingly helped to strengthen the Christians by telling them that if they were going to follow Father's way they had to follow

it `straight'. This was no doubt an attempt to identi-
fy each person's convictions in regard to killing.

The strong value placed on personal independence
and loyalty to family has kept everyone living with
their own relatives no matter whether the family is
basically Christian or basically traditional. Christianity has not produced a polarization within families, nor between communities. Non-Christians, even
today, are still on the lookout for enemies whom they
can justifiably attack. Nevertheless they appreciate
the advantages which have come to them through the
more peaceful life-style, namely, the privilege of
living to raise their children to adulthood and the
freedom to travel in safety.

The question of spirit power

Life-preserving spirit power remained a question
in the minds of Candoshi Christians for several years.
The subject of spirit power was hardly mentioned to
SIL workers who, at the time, had only the vaguest
ideas of its importance in the culture. They assumed
that since its violent manifestations had subsided, it
was probably no longer relevant, at least among Christians. The Christians, however, wanting to follow
Father's way, still desperately felt the need of sus-
taining spirit power in order to remain invulnerable
to attack. They continued, therefore, to strictly observe all the taboos that went along with the preservation of power.

In 1967, The Acts of the Apostles was translated
into Candoshi and several Christians gathered for a
final review of the manuscript prior to publication.
Candoshi courtesy does not insist that only one person
speak at a time, but rather allows two or three to
speak while the rest evaluate what each speaker is
saying. Discussions, therefore, are always lively and,
for an outsider, difficult to follow. Eighteen chap-
ters of Acts were discussed and necessary adjustments
made.

During the reading of the nineteenth chapter,
however, the group suddenly became silent. The translator was surprised but, as he had no idea what was
going on in the minds of the men, he kept on reading
to the end of verse twenty. When he stopped to wait

for comments, one man asked why the Ephesian Christians had burned their scrolls on sorcery and had not sold them. He answered that they obviously had not wanted to encourage others to practice witchcraft; they had wanted to end it completely. Again there was silence. One of the men finally said, "If we want to really follow Father's way we will have to do that also. We had better take time to think about this."

The checking session broke up at that point until the following day. Later that same day some of the men expressed their fears to the translator who had not been fully aware of the significance of spirit power beliefs in the culture. He assured them that Father was well able to take care of them. They agreed among themselves to trust their lives to Father and not depend on the evil spirits to defend them. The word spread among the Christians and gradually a much greater openness was evident throughout the group.

Since shamanism performed through the spirit anaconda was considered to be the work of evil spirits (yashinko), the people turned more to herbal remedies and patent medicines as cures for their illnesses. Most of the diseases attributed to the entering of the spirit anaconda are now associated with intestinal parasites or amoebic infections and treated accordingly. Most sudden deaths are still associated with bewitching shamanism and non-Christians still attempt to take the life of the shaman involved.

The last killing of a Candoshi shaman took place in 1975. A group of men enlisted from four different communities attacked and killed a shaman and his four sons in revenge for the death of two children. Relatives of the shaman, however, claim that he only practiced curing shamanism and the incident has resulted in very bitter feelings towards the killers. As most of the relatives of the shaman are Christians, the killing will probably not be revenged. The leader of the raid was killed during the attack.

The world view of Christian Candoshi may be summarized as follows:

1. Father has come into a preeminent position. His home in the upper world is open to all spirits of the dead who follow his way in this world.

2. Spirits of the dead who did not follow Father's way still wander aimlessly in the forest and attempt to communicate through birds and animals.

3. Evil spirits are as numerous and harmful as ever, but Father protects his people from the power of the evil spirits and from the appearances of evil spirits in phantom form.

4. Thunder and earthquakes are still feared although not so strongly associated with phantoms.

5. Rainbow people still live in the rivers but are seldom seen. Candoshi mainly travel now by outboard motor giving plenty of warning of their approach.

6. Spirit power is still pursued by some, but not by Christians.

In the early 1970's, two anthropologists visited the Candoshi and the Shapras, apparently making an effort to persuade them to return to their ancestral beliefs and customs. The people were at first puzzled and then angered when they interpreted the anthropologists as seriously suggesting that they go back to their former practice of head-hunting. Talking to us later about the incident, Shiniki Totarika of the Pushaga River summed up his feelings by saying,

> If they were serious they must think that we are not human beings. When my mother's brother was killed, mother was forced to carry his head in a basket to the home of her captives. Do they think that people can enjoy living like that? We are people; we have hearts just like everyone else.

OTHER CHANGES

A number of other cultural changes have occurred, specifically in respect to human relations within the family. Some of these changes are as follows:

Widows and orphans

Widows and orphans have traditionally been treated as slaves in Candoshi society. Several years ago, as I was trying to encourage a family to take better care of a tiny orphan girl who had been left in their care, one of the women said to me, "We are taught to make orphans and widows suffer, not to love them." One reason behind this attitude seems to be that it is a disgrace to be dependent.

Candoshi children belong to their father and his family. When a man dies, leaving dependent children, these children are divided among his relatives and his widow is sent back to live with her closest male relative.

Orphaned boys must live in the home of a female relative and are therefore usually assigned to the care of a paternal aunt. As the aunt has a natural affection for her brother's son she tends to treat him well, but he must work hard to earn his food and clothing.

Orphaned girls are sent to live either with paternal grandparents or a paternal uncle. They tend to be treated kindly by grandparents; but in the home of an uncle, they become his wife's servants. A child old enough to work hard is an acceptable addition to the household, but no one will show her affection. Her food consists of scraps left by the family and her clothes are worn-out rags. A child not old enough to work and take care of herself is not a welcome addition to a household. Her uncle still assigns her to the care of his wife as a servant, but a servant too young to work is just an added burden to an already overworked mother.

An uncle's wife is unrelated (tonari), and has no natural responsibility for the physical well-being of the child. No one, therefore, holds her responsible if the child dies. If she ill-treats the child her husband will not normally interfere; she is her servant. Being undernourished the child succumbs to any illness which comes along and is left to die. We are aware of seven cases which followed this pattern in the 1950's and early 60's.

Unless her parents are living, a widow likewise becomes the servant of her brother's wife and a family slave. The family appropriates any means she may have of providing for her own needs, such as poultry or garden produce. Widows frequently suffered from malnutrition and abuse. A Shapra woman, telling me of the death of her widowed sister, said that when her sister became too weak to work she was locked in a shed and given no food until she died. A widow could only expect freedom in another marriage.

When the Epistle of James was translated into Candoshi in the late 1960's, the people read for themselves that Father expects his people to treat widows and orphans kindly as their suffering is already great (James 1:27). SIL personnel had told the people this before with very little change in the situation. When they actually read it for themselves, however, they agreed that, if this was what Father wanted, they would have to do something about it.

Since that time only two men with dependent children have died. In the first case arrangements were made for the widow to stay in the community of her husband with her children since she had a cousin living there who offered to be responsible for her. She also had a twelve-year-old orphaned nephew living with her who hunted for the family. In the second case similar arrangements were made, but two months later the widow eloped with another man. The grandparents are now caring for the children.

Future arrangements for widows and orphans will have to be worked out with the relatives involved, but primary consideration is now being given to the well-being of the children. Non-Christians agree that this is a worthwhile cultural change. Some of them remember their own suffering as orphans.

Husband and wife relationships

Polygyny is common among the Candoshi. War chiefs often had several wives from women captured in raids, and there is no doubt that it was, and still is, prestigious for a man to have at least two wives. The treatment of wives varies greatly from one household to another. A man with a violent disposition could keep his whole family in constant fear of death. In 1969 we visited a young friend who had been given in marriage to a war chief. We found the girl living in mortal fear of her husband who, while we were there, came home, beat her across the back with his gun and threatened to kill her. This was a daily routine. A man was expected to kill his wife if he knew that she had committed adultery, but it was also not unknown for a wife to be killed by an angry drunken husband. The Shapra women told me of a woman whose husband shot her in both legs and left her to die on a jungle trail just because he was angry with her. This, of course, was an exceptional case but on the whole men treated their wives as servants and referred to them as such (no mchachori `my servant´). An exception to this is found among old men who may refer to their wives as `my dog´ (no tomoziri). This term of endearment, possibly derived from the `companion´ meaning-component of the word dog, is used only when a couple have lived together for a long time.

Father´s word is full of exhortations to husbands and wives, but the culmination of them all states, "Husbands, love your wives with the same love that Christ gave to the church when he sacrificed himself for her" (Ephesians 5:25). The initial reaction of the men to this was one of incredulity. When they were convinced that it was not a mistranslation, as they had originally thought, they decided that they could, at least, think about it. Again this has affected non-Christians who are appropriating this aspect of Father´s way to their own family situations. I was recently told that the husband of our young friend "now loves her a little bit, and does not beat her any more since Father says that it is good to love your wife."

Infanticide

The Candoshi practiced infanticide with the specific purpose of balancing the male and female population. A man usually kept daughters only in proportion to the number of his sons. He more readily tolerated an excessive number of sons, but the ideal family was, and still is, one well-balanced, with an equal number of male and female children.

The strangling of unwanted infants stopped in the late 1950´s. By the middle of the 1960´s female children greatly outnumbered the males. Ultimately, this did not cause a major problem as all but two of these girls are now married. Most were taken as first wives, four as second wives and one as a third wife.

Today an excessive number of male Shapra children
give cause for concern that they may not all be able
to obtain spouses among their own people. One family
has ten sons and no daughters, and two other families
each have six sons and one daughter. Only time will
tell how this problem will be resolved.

UNCHANGED CUSTOMS AND VALUES

The above social adjustments have not changed the
internal social structure of the group. All kinship
customs and responsibilities are still carried out to
the full. The basic kinship group is still a man, his
parents, his siblings, his children and his brothers'
children. Marriage arrangements still include traditional exchange or bride service to the father or
brother of the bride. Polygyny is still common, but
not as prevalent as when women were the spoil of
warfare.

The two highest social values continue to be as
before (1) the self-reliance of the adult male, and
(2) loyalty to family. All Candoshi life revolves
around these two values.

Government is neither in the hands of one individual nor of a group of individuals. Decisions concerning a household are made by the men of the household.
Decisions concerning a community, whether an extended-
family or multiple-family community, are made by con-
sensus, older men usually carrying more weight than
younger men. Those who do not agree with a majority
decision simply go their own way. They do not criti-
cize those who made the decision, nor do others put
pressure on them to conform. Each man is a free
individual.

Perhaps this characteristic, more than any other,
has been the strength of the Candoshi culture over the
past twenty years of ever-increasing contact with the
outside world. Their respect for individual diversity
carries over into their dealings with people of other
cultures. If outsiders are slow to concede to them the
same privilege, they do what they want to do anyway.

Traditional chiefs were exclusively war chiefs,
and their prestige lasted only as long as they were
successful in battle. As a prerequisite to being a war

chief, a man had to be a powerful and persuasive speaker. This aspect of leadership has carried over into `postwar´ society. Those who aspire to chieftain-ship recognize the value of forceful speech and over the years we have noticed that those who have the wisdom to evaluate situations and present advice per-suasively come to be recognized, to some extent, as chiefs. Those who are purely loquacious but add little to the discussion gradually fall back into the general rank and file of the people.

Visiting is as much a part of the daily schedule as work or hunting. Three to four hours every day in the late afternoon and evening are given to intercom-munity visiting just to chat or discuss community problems. Periodic visits are made to relatives who live on other rivers, the frequency of visits being determined by the closeness of the relationship.

These basic customs and social values still strongly hold Candoshi society together. The security and strength of the society has enabled the people to relate increasingly to the outside world without any desire to become an integral part of it.

CONCLUDING REMARKS

A summary of the events recorded in this paper, regarding Candoshi behavioral change, is as follows:

1. The Candoshi have traditionally been theists.

2. Conflict and factionalism were rapidly de-stroying the Candoshi as a people.

3. The New Testament, translated into the verna-cular, expanded the Candoshi view of God as a God of love.

4. A leading war chief made a moral decision to obey the words of God as found in the New Testament.

5. When he refused to revenge his own injuries and the death of his brother-in-law, his enemies were convinced that he was no longer a threat to them.

6. Others became Christians. Gradually most of the killings stopped because the Christians were no

longer a threat to their enemies.

7. Other social changes have been made by the Candoshi with a view to reducing suffering.

8. Many aspects of Candoshi culture remain essentially unchanged.

It is popular in some circles to consider the introduction of conservative Christianity into an indigenous, non-Western culture as a divisive influence, resulting in conflict and factionalism which--as some would have us believe--is not traditionally a significant factor in such communities. This study documents a case to the contrary.

Anne-Christine Taylor, in an article entitled "God-Wealth: The Achuar and the Missions" (1981:650-52), looks at the present day Achuar situation from a materialistic point of view and suggests that the Achuar allowed "mission policies to take root within the very core of the culture" as an attempt (1) to reestablish new sources of foreign goods, (2) to perpetuate the prestige of the Achuar great men who were using white goods to strengthen their social position, and (3) to take advantage of the presence of white men as a protection from war raids, especially as the white men stressed peace. None of these considerations related to the Candoshi situation. Perhaps Taylor, unwilling to accept a nonmaterialistic answer to questions she posed, failed to look deeply enough into the moral and ethical factors of Achuar life which may have contributed to their social change. Even anthropologists must certainly admit that man may be motivated by more than materialistic considerations.

There is an interesting parallel between the Candoshi culture and that of the Western Dani. Heider (1975:60-66), following a comparative study of the Western Dani and the Grand Valley Dani cultures, proposes that the Western Dani, who wholeheartedly accepted Christianity, were an 'individual-intensifying' society with a weak social structure and a relatively high degree of cultural stress, and that these factors possibly predisposed them to accept cultural change. These same features were very strongly present in Candoshi society, a difference, however, being that not all the Candoshi have accepted Christianity.

Predisposing factors to change, however, do not constitute motives for change. In order to accept a radical change in behavior such as Christianity brings to a society, people must be convinced that the new beliefs are `good´, as defined by their own value system. In the case of the Candoshi, we suspect that some have rejected Christianity because they prefer the old way of power and prestige or because they do not want to forgive old grievances. Nevertheless many non-Christian Candoshi have altered their lifestyle to some extent in deference to Christianity in that it is not at variance with their own value system.

Politics aside, few will disagree that the teachings of the Bible have been beneficial to the Candoshi people, eliminating a high percentage of the violence and suffering among them. Candoshi culture nevertheless remains intact. The Candoshi people continue to be proud of their traditions and appear to be determined to continue in a way of life of their own choosing. Whether or not they will be allowed to do so in this world of political turmoil remains to be seen.

NOTE

[1]The Candoshi are often mistakenly referred to as Muratos (Muratas) by mestizos of the Pastaza River area. The Muratos, according to the Candoshi, were an Andoan group who lived around the Lake Rimachi and Pastaza River area and who are now extinct. It seems probable that the Candoshi, being the only indigenous people left in that area, were thought to be Muratos by outsiders. This would explain the confusion over the linguistic identification of Candoshi expressed by Stewart (1948:629,635).

Neither are the Candoshi synonymous with the Maina. The Shapra claim to have annihilated the last of the Mainas, a group who resided on the lower Morona River, probably during the latter half of the 19th Century.

REFERENCES

Descolas, Phillippe. 1981. From scattered to nucleated settlement: a process of socioeconomic change among the Achuar. In Norman E. Whitten, Jr.

(ed.), Cultural transformations and ethnicity in modern Ecuador, pp. 614-46. Urbana: University of Illinois Press.

Harner, Michael J. 1972. The Jivaro. New York: Anchor Press/Doubleday.

Heider, Karl G. 1975. Societal intensification and cultural stress. Oceania 46:53-67.

Karsten, Rafael. 1923. Blood revenge, war and victory feasts among the Jivaro Indians of Eastern Ecuador. Bureau of American Ethnology bulletin 79. Washington: Smithsonian Institution.

Steward, Julian H. 1948. Tribes of the Peruvian and Ecuadorian montaña. Handbook of South American Indians, Bureau of American Ethnology bulletin 43:535-56. Washington: Smithsonian Institution.

Taylor, Anne-Christine. 1981. God-wealth: the Achuar and the missions. In Norman E. Whitten, Jr. (ed.), Cultural transformations and ethnicity in modern Ecuador, pp. 647-76. Urbana: University of Illinois Press.

Wallis, Ethel E. 1965. Tariri: my story. New York: Harper and Row.

Whitten, Norman E., Jr. 1981. Amazonia today at the base of the Andes: an ethnic interface in ecology, social and ideological perspectives. In Norman E. Whitten, Jr. (ed.), Cultural transformations and ethnicity in modern Ecuador, pp. 121-61. Urbana: University of Illinois Press.

WATER, ROCK, AND SMOKE:

A GUANANO VIEW OF THE WORLD

Carolyn Waltz

Summer Institute of Linguistics, Colombia

"Three things on this earth do not
die," explained the Guanano shaman, "water,
rock, and smoke." Mandu himself lay dying in
his hammock, and so his thoughts turned
toward life and death. This one statement
embodies the three levels of the Guanano
view of the world--the world of water, the
world of rock, and the world of sky.

This paper[1] addresses the Guanano world view,
including the nature of the universe and the nature of
man. Guanano ritual specialists of the Vaupés region
of Colombia, South America, traditionally character-
ized the world in terms of these three eternal veri-
ties--water, rock, and smoke--each with its own spatial and social realities. These elements not only
figured in Guanano origins, but are also associated
with (1) the important beings Anaconda, Jaguar, and
Eagle, and (2) particular classes of persons which the
ritual specialist must attempt to control. The Guanano
person called Bisiu, of the realm of smoke, is found
to be the same as the legendary Yurupary spoken of by
Goldman (1963) and Hugh-Jones (1974). Dietary restrictions placed on the specialist, the ill feelings of
those who fear his power, and the strain of heavy case
loads are found to be combining with modernizing

factors such as materialism to undermine the stability
of this traditional view.

The Guananos are a culturally homogeneous language group numbering some 1000 persons who inhabit

the Vaupés River region from Santa Cruz, below Mitú, Colombia, to Yavaraté in Brazil. The Guanano language belongs to the Eastern Tucanoan family (Waltz and Wheeler 1972). The Guanano practice hunting, fishing, and horticulture in a tropical rain forest and wide Vaupés River setting (Waltz 1973). The Vaupés River can be classified as a clear water river. Its banks are high and stable, and the river amply supports a supply of many kinds of fish. Between Santa Cruz and Yabaraté there are more than forty large rapids.

The Guananos practice slash and burn agriculture, preferring bitter cassava as their staple food. They call themselves People of the Water and are much more at home when traveling by canoe than when traveling on foot through the forest. They much prefer fishing, a main part of their daily routine, to hunting, a more incidental activity.

The Guanano people constitute a phratry of patrilineal sibs, of which there are approximately thirteen, the number varying from speaker to speaker. Each sib is ranked according to the order in which its respective mythical ancestor emerged from the ancestral canoe (or otherwise appeared on earth), which brings us to the discussion of the first level of the Guanano view of the world, the world of water.

Much of the detail which follows in regard to Guanano world view is taken from an unpublished text dictated by Candi Melo in 1975.

Water

Water figures prominently in the Guanano creation myth, and is almost a world in itself. It was the vehicle through which the Ancestral People (Pahmoni Masa) traveled to their present locations in the Vaupés region. The Ancestral People were created by Cohamacu down at Wapãri Duri, below Yavaraté in Brazil. The Guanano Ancestors ascended the Vaupés River in Ancestral Canoe (Pjahmori busoca), also known as Anaconda Canoe (Pjinono Busoca), disembarking at the hole in the rock at Santa Cruz. Anaconda Canoe then continued to travel back down the Vaupés River, letting off people at various locations--at the headwaters of various tributaries and other rivers.

Christine Hugh-Jones (1979) speaks of many anacondas bringing the Ancestral People of the Barasana to their present locations, but the Guananos speak of a single Ancestral Canoe or Anaconda.

One person told me that the Ancestors emerged from a hole in the rock at Santa Cruz and were given gifts by Cohamacu. All the Ancestors were frightened except Barea, who received a gun as his gift and became the ancestor of the non-indigenous peoples (hereinafter referred to as `foreigners'). The hole in the rock from which the Guanano and other peoples of the Vaupés region emerged can still be viewed during low water.

The Guanano Ancestors emerged by rank. Cjene, Captain of Ancestral Canoe, emerged first, founding the highest ranking sib, Cjenoa. The Guananos settled in the best area, along the banks of the large Vaupés River. Other language groups settled mainly on the tributaries to the Vaupés and on other rivers, the Cubeo settling along the Querari River, and the Desano along the Abiyu.

The order of emergence of Guanano ancestors after Cjene, as generally understood by present-day Guananos (including Candi Melo), is as follows:

> Biari,
> Wahi Cape Najori Pohna,
> Najori Pohna,
> Muhria Najori Pohna,
> Bueri Najori Pohna,
> Diana Pohna,
> Bahtiroca Pohna,
> Neteno Wisocu Pohna,
> Nitidusoria,
> Naharia, and
> Docana.

The Wiroa sib arrived later, on the backs of birds, and were originally considered to be servants.

Each sib is ranked according to the order in which its ancestor emerged. Members of each sib refer to members of lower ranking sibs as `younger brothers' and to members of higher ranking sibs as `older brothers'.

There is some difference of opinion as to the
order of emergence of the Ancestors, depending upon
the sib membership of the source. Only Cjene and Biari
were mentioned by Candi Melo in his 1975 formal text
on the subject. There seems to be a tendency to
ascribe higher rank to one's own sib than to those of
others. Statements are heard about other sibs, such
as, "They think they are higher, but we are truly
higher." There is general agreement, however, that
Cjene was Captain and of highest rank and Biari the
second. Only one member of Cjene's sib now remains,
and he has moved away from Guanano territory.

It is also generally agreed that the Wiroa sib is
the lowest, and that they were originally servants.
When we lived in Villa Fátima, however, where the
highest concentration of Wiroa now live, they told me
that they ranked highest among the sibs.

Not only does water figure prominently in the
origins of the Guanano people; it also figures in
their view of today's world. The world of water is
where the Fish People (Wahi Masa) live. The Guananos
call themselves People of the Water, but this is a
very different order of beings from Fish People, whom
Cohamacu originally placed in the rivers. The House of
Fish People (Wahi Masa Wuhu) is located deep in the
water, and Anaconda is their grandfather just as the
Ancestral Peoples who emerged from Anaconda, or Ancestral Canoe, are the grandfathers of the present-day
sibs.

Fish People's House is said to be very beautiful,
but also dangerous. If a Guanano were to visit and eat
there, the Fish People would take him and keep him. A
Fish Man (Wahi Masuno) may also take a Guanano woman
as his wife. A Guanano woman needs special protection
from Fish People if she travels on the water during
her menses. She, therefore, paints red spots on her
face during that time. A young girl who is experienc-
ing her first menses must paint her entire face red in
order to afford greater protection for herself during
this time which is particularly dangerous for her.

Because of the danger which exists from Fish
People, the Guanano people bathe ceremonially in the
river, especially after the birth of a child or after
a girl's first menses. Through proper ritual during
ceremonial bathing, preceded by many hours of chanting

by the elders, an individual is protected and is able
to bathe safely thereafter.

The chanting by the elders during such times is
directed toward Ancestral Woman (Pahmori Masono), down
at Milk Lake (Chernela 1982). Ancestral Woman was one
of the original Ancestors along with Wanari Cohamacu.
These two are Rock People (Tã Masa) and were created
by Thunder before the Guananos or Ancestral Canoe
existed. Ancestral Woman is also known as Milk Woman
(Pẽcho Masono). She originally came upriver from Milk
Lake, stopping at each village where, by blowing sacred tobacco smoke, she put Fish People to sleep so
that they would not harm the Guananos. Now the elders
chant to her and blow sacred tobacco smoke, thereby
putting Fish People to sleep and reducing harmful
influences in the river.

Fish People are light-complected like foreigners.
When they come up from their house, however, they
clothe themselves in anaconda skins, which permits
them to appear, at times, as anacondas.

All foreigners are suspected of being Fish People. When we sit down to our table and eat off plates,
with forks, it does not surprise the Guanano people at
all. "That is just what it is like in Fish People's
House," they say. "They have tables, plates, forks,...
everything, just like you."

Fish People figure prominently in Guanano mythology. The ancestor Wanari Cohamacu created his consort
out of a tree. They had conflicts, however, and he
killed her. He later took Anaconda Woman, also known
as Piranha Woman (Buhu Masono), to be his wife, but
found it very difficult to live at Fish People's
House. It was dangerous to visit his father-in-law.
Not only did anacondas crawl all over him, trying to
kill him, but the piranhas tried to eat him as well.
Only by calling fish-eating birds to help him was he
able to escape. His union with Anaconda Woman did not
last long.

Next he found a beautiful Guanano girl to be his
wife, whom he taught how to plant bitter cassava,
planting the first field miraculously. Unfortunately
his mother-in-law ruined everything by speaking during
the miraculous growth process. When she spoke, weeds
began to grow and the cassava became covered with a

hard peeling which all Guanano women must now laboriously remove. Wanari Cohamacu also taught his wife to process the bitter cassava so that Guananos can safely eat the delicious cassava bread today. He also taught her to make the first fermented cassava beer. Wanari Cohamacu had passed through the first level of the Guanano world, the world of water, where he had married Anaconda Woman, before he moved on to teach the first Guananos in the second world of rock and land, where the Guananos live.

In summary, the world of water figures prominently in Guanano origins, as well as in present-day activities, such as chanting to Milk Woman, blowing ceremonial tobacco, and ceremonial bathing to protect them from Fish People.

Rock

Rock represents the second level of the Guanano world, the land on which the Guanano people live. It, too, figures prominently in Guanano origins. It is said that rock existed before the first Guanano appeared on earth. Large rock formations along the Vaupés River chronicle Guanano prehistory, each major formation signifying a particular event. As mentioned above, for example, Ancestral Canoe traveled to the rock formation at Santa Cruz where the Guanano sibs came into existence.

Another formation, at Villa Fátima, is associated with a legendary flood. When flood waters began to rise, the Guananos rushed to climb this huge rock which emerges from the jungle floor. The women, who were all standing together on one side of the rock mountain, became so frightened that they began jumping up and down in terror, causing their side of the rock to sink. And thus, today, the rock of Villa Fátima has one hump much lower than the other.

Just as Fish People are associated with the level of water, so Rock People are associated with the level of rock. Rock people were created long ago, at the same time as Wanari Cohamacu, but after the sun, moon, and stars had appeared. They were formed from Diroa Cohamana when the latter were changed into rock by being struck by Lightning. The grandmother of the Rock

People became a rock down at Yavaraté, which is shaped like a pot.

One Rock Person, named Piraduca, threatened Ancestral Canoe as it came upriver with the Ancestral People aboard. The Rock People wanted to destroy Ancestral Canoe, but were unable to do so. Piraduca himself was killed by Baleiro, a foreigner from down near San Gabriel, in Brazil. Huge outcroppings of rock called Wariroca are also to be found near San Gabriel. These are said to be the houses where Wanari Cohamaca and his brother Churi Bo now live.

Rock People, as such, no longer exist; only the rocks remain. They have become the entrances into the earth where other beings of the level of Rock live. Since Rock People do not interact with or threaten the Guananos today, the Guanano shaman need do nothing to protect the Guanano people from them.

The beings which now reside inside these rock outcroppings are known as Jungle Beings (Macaraca Macaina). These beings are very important to the Guanano people; the shaman spends a great deal of time attempting to control their activities. Jungle Beings are of various types, one of which is Animal Souls (Wahiquina Yajeripohnari).

Animal Souls live inside rock formations in their Animal Houses (Wahiquina Wuhuse), souls of every kind of animal. Most of these souls are benign; but Boraro, Chief of Animal Souls, is dangerous, as is another one named Wahi Wai Yoro, who whips people and takes them to his house. The jaguar has the strongest soul of all the animals (Stephen Hugh-Jones 1972), and is said to be dangerous because he eats people. For the most part, however, the residents of Animal Soul Houses do not harm people.

The Guanano shaman, then, tries to exercise authority over these Animal Souls. Through the use of a special type of quartz crystal (wijŏ), he can open the door of the Animal Soul House to release animals into the forest so that the Guanano people can hunt and be assured of meat. The wijŏ is also used to kill people, and this use of wijŏ is considered dangerous; the user may have to pay a price for its use, such as the life of a child, often someone close to the shaman or even of his own family. The people say that it is for this reason that Chief Ricardo had no sons, since, in his role as shaman, he had used the wijõ power.

A shaman must not eat chili peppers for an entire year after having smelled the wijõ quartz. If he does, someone will die. After a year of not eating peppers, the shaman must chant for an entire day. Only then may he safely begin to eat them again. The shaman may sniff the quartz in April, and perhaps again in August. Then he must wait until the following year before he can eat chili peppers again.

The houses of the dead are also in these large rock outcroppings. Each language group has its own house of the dead. There are two houses of the dead for Guananos. One is named Buhi Cohto 'high place' and is near the village of Matapi. The other is at the village of Cemeteria and is named Buca Turu Nuco 'old generation island'.

The souls of deceased Guananos go to a house for the dead, located in the earth, unless the deceased had been particularly evil in life. In such a case, the soul would just stay at the grave and is called a Devil Soul (Watíno Yajeripohna) that menaces the living. The Guanano house of the dead can also be called a Devil-arrival House (Watí Cohari Wuhu). Guananos say that conditions are good in this region.

Guananos are not afraid of the departed Souls whom they consider benign, for example, those of children. When a child dies, the body may be buried right in the floor of the house, "so that the child will not get wet when it rains."

When an older person dies, on the other hand, particularly a shaman, there is great fear. In former times, the shaman would be buried in the floor of the communal maloca (longhouse) where he lived, and the maloca was then burned to the ground.

Devil Souls return to bother the living. If an object crashes to the ground from the rafters of a house, it is the work of a Devil Soul which has come back to cause trouble. In such an instance, someone from the house or community will often take a gourd bowl of chili peppers in boiling water around the house and even outside, so that the steam from the chilis will drive the evil influences away.

To summarize, the world of water is where the anaconda is the strongest creature and is the place where Fish People live; while the world of rock, where Rock People formerly lived, is where Animal Houses and houses of the dead are located. The shaman not only concerns himself with protecting the Guanano people from Fish People in the river, but must also concern himself with Animal Souls to ensure that there will be enough game in the forest for the coming year, as well as to protect the Guananos from Devil Souls which might return to menace them.

Smoke

The third level in the Guanano world is that of smoke, or of the sky. As the shaman smokes the sacred tobacco smoke, he makes contact with the world of the sky; as the smoke rises into the sky, he makes contact with the beings of that realm.

One of the more important of these beings is Father of Eagles (Cja Bucu). He is a very large and fierce eagle, known also as Sky Shaman. Sky Shaman eats people. When a shaman communes with the inhabitants of Sky House, he must smoke the sacred tobacco. As the smoke rises to the sky, it puts Sky Shaman to sleep, permitting the Guanano shaman's soul to safely enter Sky House to find out whatever it is that he needs to learn from Bisiu, Chief of Devils. Then, having secured the needed information, the shaman's soul leaves Sky House, after which he allows Sky Shaman to awaken.

Bisiu, Chief of Devils, is another resident of Sky House and the world of smoke. He introduced the first fruit-sharing dance (pohoa) to the Guanano, the Yurupary dance. When doing so, however, he became very angry with some little boys who were bothering him. In his anger, he killed the boys. As a result, the first Guananos became so angry that they built a huge bonfire and burned him. As his body burned, it ascended in smoke to the sky, where he is today. The first poisons grew in the ashes of that bonfire and, today, Bisiu is in charge of all cursings, poisonings, and other such bad activities.

Whenever a shaman puts Sky Shaman to sleep, he is free to enter Sky House and commune with Bisiu so as to find a cure for a sickness or a solution for whatever problem he is dealing with. In order to do this, the shaman not only smokes the sacred tobacco, but must also take a hallucinogen (capi banisterium; Shultz 1978) to free his own soul to travel to Sky House. In more difficult cases, he may also sniff the sacred quartz crystal (wijõ). There are other types of wijõ power as well--vines and leaves which can be made into a liquid.

I was recently surprised to discover that Bisiu is the Guanano name for the legendary Yurupary (Goldman 1963; Hugh-Jones 1974, 1979). Although I have never seen the initiation dance in which Yurupary is supposed to appear, from talking with Guanano men I get a slightly different picture from that which Stephen Hugh-Jones (1976) painted for the Barasana. He suggests that space and time are compressed in Tucanoan thinking and that the entire history of the group becomes compressed in the consciousness of its members into a period of two generations. It thus becomes necessary, when the Yurupary dance takes place, for young boys to be initiated into membership in the community through an introduction to the ancestors who are summoned to the dance by the playing of the sacred horns, one of the ancestors being Yurupary himself.

I tend to get a different picture in talking with Guananos. The evil Bisiu is Yurupary in the Guanano language. He was the one who ate some Guanano boys during the preparations for the first Yurupary dance. As the Guananos have explained it to me, during the Yurupary dance, they summon Bisiu by the playing of the sacred horns, and he comes with all his demons (watîa) and all the women must flee lest they die. I understand the dance to be one in which the young boys being initiated into manhood are forced to stand up to the fearsome Bisiu. In showing bravery--staying in the house where all the demons have entered--each boy shows his courage and, thus, his qualifications for manhood. This contrasts with the idea of being introduced to the ancestors.

Janet Chernela[2] was with us among the Guananos when the connection was made between Bisiu and Yurupary, and she also confirmed this in her own studies. I believe she witnessed an initiation ceremony at our location. Perhaps her studies when published will reveal more on this interesting point.

Bisiu is also called Thunder Cohamacʉ (Wʉpo Cohamacʉ), and is Chief of the Guardians of Wijõ, who are
other residents of Sky House, also known as Thunder
House (Wʉpo ya Wʉhʉ), where Sky Shaman lives.

When a Guanano becomes ill, it is because his
soul has wandered away. By the use of wijõ and the
capi hallucinogen, a shaman is able to obtain another
soul from the Chief of Wijõ to replace the one that
was lost.

A person may lose his soul in sleep, through
sickness, or because of a cursing and thus eventually
die as a result. There is a payment involved in the
acquisition of a new soul, and this is the cause of a
great deal of trouble in the Vaupés. No death is
accidental. Death is usually considered the direct
result of violating a taboo, such as looking at a
menstruating woman. In such a case, the woman's uncon-
ceived child steals the soul of the man who saw the
woman so that the child will have a soul. Since no
misfortune is an accident, the shaman is kept busy
communing with the residents of Sky House in an attempt to resolve these problems.

There are many parallels between the three levels
of water, rock, and smoke. First, they all figure in
Guanano origins: water in relation to Ancestral Canoe,
rock in the legendary history of the rock formations,
and smoke, in the introduction of the Yurupary dance
and creation of poisons after Bisiu was burned and
ascended to the sky. Secondly, each level has a particular animal which predominates: Anaconda, grandfather of Fish People and the most powerful being in
the world of water; jaguar, the most fearsome animal
of the world of land and rock, the one whose soul the
shaman takes; and Eagle, the Sky Shaman, Guardian of
Thunder House, where Bisiu, the fearsome Chief of
Devils lives. Lastly, each level is populated by
beings whom the shaman must control--Water People,
Souls of Animals and of the Dead, and sky beings like
the Guardians of wijõ.

I now turn to the Guanano view of man.

Man

Man is made up of a body, which dies, and a soul
(yajeripohna 'breath-offspring'), which may separate

from it. The soul makes a person kind, congenial, and well-liked. It makes him compassionate. Yajeri means `breath'. When Wanari Cohamacu created his first wife out of a tree, he `breathed' life into her, giving her his own soul (yajeripohna).

We once observed a dead child who had drowned in the river. His father, a shaman, circled the dead boy's body for hours, blowing tobacco smoke over him, trying in vain to breathe life back into him by re- placing the `soul' he had lost in the act of drowning.

The souls of all peoples are not alive. Foreign- ers have souls but they are not with them on this earth, as are those of the Guanano people. This is why foreigners suffer less sickness than Guananos do. The first rubber workers who entered the area were looking for slave labor and were a cruel lot (Cifuentes 1979:97). One older Guanano man said his father had been strung up by his thumbs from the rafters of a maloca for not cooperating with them. This kind of behavior has undoubtedly contributed to the belief that foreigners do not have a soul--the seat of conge- niality and compassion.

The soul is moral. When a Guanano does wrong, they say that "he does not feel his soul." When he is uncongenial or does not get along with others, they say that "his soul is not functioning well." Love, hate, and desire are all felt with the soul, as is homesickness.

Each person has just one soul, which leaves the body at death. It may also become separated from the body when a person sleeps.

The term yajeripohna is also used in reference to the heart as a physical organ. Since the heart is located near the stomach, this area is considered the seat of the emotions. Many emotive terms, in Guanano, have the root for stomach (pja) in them, such as pja ñu `to have mercy'.

Animals also have a yajeripohna, different spe- cies having souls of different strengths. The jaguar and the danta have very strong souls. These same animals also have intelligence and compassion. The anteater has a child's soul and not much intelligence. He is unable to think (tuho masierara). The sloth has a soul, but no intelligence. The anaconda has a soul, but no compassion. A certain kind of frog without intestines (pjahta) is about the only animal that has no soul.

In contrast with the soul, spirits (bajueraina `not-appearing-ones´), of which there are many kinds, are quite different. Some spirits live in trees in the forest, where there are no people. Such spirits are generally bad. Some spirits are very strong, others not. Many are like people, in that they eat. Bad spirits in the forest squeeze people to death, sucking out their insides through their ears. There is one good spirit, named Mácucu, who no longer kills people, although he used to do so.

There are a variety of other kinds of spirits as well. Dwarf-like spirits called cjöjécu live in the forest and eat people. Sü diroa live in trees, caves, and rocks; they do not eat people. Nehneroa are very powerful, and live in lakes. Certain locations are recognized as the habitation of spirits. One lives right down at our bathing port, so that the Guanano seldom, if ever, bathe there.

A spirit cannot enter or leave a body at will, but may move about apart from a body. Inanimate objects may be occupied by a spirit. A sick Guanano living in our guest house was once bothered by spirits which caused his hammock to swing violently. He called them demons (watia).

A spirit can appear as a man. It can partake of fish, food, and ants, but does not cook. It squeezes its food, and kills people by squeezing them to death. A spirit cannot be controlled by man, because it does not have a soul--it cannot respond, think, or know emotion. The one way a shaman can rid a location of spirits is to carry steaming-hot chilis around in a gourd bowl. He can make them leave the location, but he cannot destroy them.

The shaman and change

The Guanano shaman system has within it the seeds of its own demise. The shaman´s role is very demanding. Now that alternatives are open to the Guanano--hospitals, modern medicine--very few young men are willing to assume the heavy burden of responsibility that the shaman must carry.

In the 1975 account of Guanano shamanism which Candi Meli dictated to us, he explained it this way:

> A good shaman is like a doctor. He smokes [tobacco] well in order to blow and the sickness passes. But then there is another kind of shaman. "I want to become the kind of shaman who kills people," he says, and so that kind of shaman sniffs the very expensive kind of wijõ. [It is expensive because it requires the life of an individual as payment for its use.] This kind of shaman is called a yai sõ shaman. When he does that, this kind of [bad] shaman causes people to become sick....This is the kind of shaman the people complain against....The people say that he kills and destroys people without cause.

By just being a shaman, a person runs the risk of being called a bad shaman whenever things go wrong and people do not get well as hoped. And if he should choose to use wijõ power, he must refrain from eating certain foods for up to a year. The shaman in Yutica was emaciated and sickly for this very reason. He spent a good deal of time at our house, receiving food and medical attention.

The shaman has a load on his shoulders which he cannot easily shift. The longer he is a shaman, the more enemies he has. People blame him for deaths that occur, saying that he has stolen souls through use of wijõ power. When he needs help himself, he has no one to turn to. Shamans in other locations are usually his adversaries, through long years of warfare over the procurement of souls for sick patients. Even his own relatives fear him.

"Who will help me?" cried one powerful shaman who came to us for medical treatment. Mandu, the shaman who as he neared his own death had said, "Three things on this earth do not die--water, rock, and smoke," in the end turned against this world view that he had served his entire life. "It's all lies," he cried, and turned instead to Christianity.

Young men are no longer being trained to be shamans. "When Chief Ricardo dies, there will be no strong shamans left on the river," I was told. Soon there will be no shamans left at all. Young men do not want to be trained or to assume the heavy burden of responsibility that the older men have carried.

A second area of change relates to the younger generation of Guanano men and women who know very little of the traditional views of their elders. As new shamans are not being trained, traditions are being lost.

We have been trying to preserve the traditional oral literature through writers' workshops, in which the Guanano people themselves record their traditions in writing and on tape. Young people, however, are becoming more and more interested in material things and less so in world view, as such. The construction of the trans-Amazonian highway in Brazil has already indirectly opened up Guanano territory to the outside world. Cocaine traffic on the Colombian side has begun to bring a new level of affluence, at least for the moment. The government of Brazil is already giving old-age pensions to Brazilian Guananos. There are now regular flights in and out of Guanano territory. The Guananos are becoming interested in having cattle, medical care, and the material goods they see when they visit towns like Mitú and Yavaraté.

Younger Guananos are losing interest in a world view that cannot offer them the goods they want. One man said, "God wanted to give the Guananos gifts when they emerged from the Ancestral Canoe, but they were afraid. As a result they only received gifts of feathers, beads, hallucinatory drink, and cassava beer. Only the white-skinned foreigners received gifts of manufactured products (pache) because they were not afraid of them."

We see in this that the Guanano world view is truly self-contained. It even accounts for the materialism that is causing young, present-day Guananos to reject that view and to go out in search of material prosperity.

NOTES

[1]This study was undertaken as part of a long-range project of the Summer Institute of Linguistics under the patronage of the Dirección General de Integración y Desarrollo de la Comunidad of the Ministry of Government of Colombia. My husband and I began language-related studies among the Guanano in 1964. My interest in Guanano world view was first guided by a questionnaire developed by my colleague Rich Mansen. Later, in 1979, Janet Chernela shared reference material she had collected, including the most helpful early study by Stephen Hugh-Jones (1972) dealing with the nearby Barasana whose cosmological framework is of the same general form as that of the Guanano. The most complete recent study of a Vaupés world view is Stephen Hugh-Jones (1979).

The data for this study were gathered over twenty years of field trips among the Guanano from 1964 to 1984. Folklore texts gathered primarily for linguistic analysis became the first basis of the study, supplemented by extended and repeated interviews with our Guanano friends. Candi Melo, an older man of Yutica (recently deceased), was my primary consultant; but Samuel Gómez (67 years) and Yerman Teixera (65 years) also helped me. I am indebted to my SIL colleague, Marion Miller, who led me to the term wijỡ through the Desana cognate.

For a description of Guanano sounds see Waltz (1976). In this paper, language forms are presented in an orthography adapted to Spanish for local use. /h/ and aspiration of stop phonemes are written with j, the palatal affricate /č/ is written as ch, /k/ as c or qu, /ɨ/ is written as u, glottal stop is written as h, and nasalization as tilde (ẽ).

[2]Janet Chernela is a Fullbright scholar who is doing a detailed study of the Guanano phratry, and more particularly of Guanano sibs and rank in relation to land use.

REFERENCES

Chernela, Janet. 1982. Song of the Pahmori Masono. Ms. in author's file.

Cifuentes, Alexander. 1979. Educación y Organización Social en el Noroeste Amazónica. Revista Colombiana de Antropología 22:85-134.

Goldman, Irving. 1963. The Cubeo Indians of the Northwest Amazon. Urbana: University of Illinois Press.

Hugh-Jones, Christine. 1979. From the Milk River: Spatial and Temporal Processes in Northwest Amazonia. Cambridge: Cambridge University Press.

Hugh-Jones, Stephen. 1972. Why Shamans Are Jaguars. Ms. in author's file.

-----. 1974. Male Initiation and Cosmology Among the Barasana Indians of the Vaupés Area of Colombia. Ph.D. Dissertation. Cambridge University.

-----. 1976. Like Leaves on the Forest Floor: Space and Time in Barasana Ritual. Paper Presented at the 42nd International Congress of Americanists, Paris.

-----. 1979. The Palm and the Pleiades: Initiation and Cosmology in Northwest Amazonia. Cambridge: Cambridge University Press.

Schultz, Richard Evans. 1978. Richard Spruce Still Lives. Hortulus Aliquando 3:13-37.

Waltz, Nathan E. and Carolyn H. Waltz. 1967. Guanano Phonemics. Phonemic Systems of Colombian Languages. Publications in Linguistics and Related Fields 14:25-36. Norman: University of Oklahoma and the Summer Institute of Linguistics.

-----. 1973. Guanano. Aspectos de la Cultura Material de Grupos Etnicos 1:125-37. Lomalinda, Meta: Instituto Lingüístico de Verano, A.C.

Waltz, Nathan and Alva Wheeler. 1972. Proto Tucanoan. Comparative Studies in Amerindian Languages. The Hague: Mouton.

NATURE AND CULTURE IN FOUR KARITIANA LEGENDS

Rachel M. Landin

Summer Institute of Linguistics, Brazil

A primary contribution of Lévi-Strauss to anthropology has been his innovative approach to the study of myth (1955, 1966, 1967, 1969). His ideas on this subject have received a wide range of responses. Yalman (1967), on the one hand, says that Lévi-Strauss has done for the study of mythology what Radcliffe-Brown did for the study of social structure, while others have criticized him (Leach 1970, Carroll 1981). I do not wish to enter into this dialogue here, but simply present a modest application of Lévi-Straussian methodology to four legends told by the Karitiana people of northwestern Brazil.[1]

One of Lévi-Strauss' main tenets is the universality of human thought mechanisms. He finds this to be supported by the occurrence of a number of universal themes in mythology from around the world. I cannot here attempt a large-scale presentation, but will show that some of these recurrent themes are in fact present and explored in Karitiana mythological thought.

I also draw upon Bastien (1979), who emphasizes the need to firmly root any analysis of myth in an ethnographic approach. We must ask of a myth, "What does this myth mean to a people in the context of their own culture?" Cognitive patterns revealed in the myth should be the same as those found in the social structure and in other cultural institutions. An understanding of myth cannot be isolated from this social context. Examining Karitiana stories, I attempt to relate their analysis to other aspects of Karitiana society to see if the same patterns are present there as well. The four stories are presented below in summary form, each with a discussion of the Lévi-Straussian themes they embody, and the paper ends with a summary of my findings.

Fire Child leaves humankind

This story tells how a young man named Ohẽy foolishly wanted to watch Fire Child (whose name is Isoason) burn a field in preparation for planting. Ohẽy should have stayed in the village, but went into the field where he died, accidentally, in the fire. Shamed by this, Fire Child separates himself from the company of humankind in the village by going out to live alone in the jungle. He leaves a song behind which the Karitiana can use each year to summon him when it is time to burn their fields.

The physical setting of this story is a field which lies between the village (culture) and the jungle (nature). The field is temporarily drawn into the realm of culture by the application of fire (by `cooking´ the earth).

In the area of economics, burning the field is implicitly contrasted with what would happen if the field were not burned--there would be no food and the Karitiana would go hungry. Food produced by horticulture is more certain than food supplied by hunting. Horticultural foods are under man´s control if he can burn the jungle to make it suitable for planting. The field is thus contrasted with the jungle, and the solitary presence of Fire in the field is contrasted with Man in the village. Fire exercises strong, uncontrolled power in the field while Man waits passively in the village. Fire is the mediator, transforming the jungle into a field and making possible both the production of horticultural food and culture.

In the area of social organization, we see a gradual separation of fire from culture. The story begins with Fire living with people in culture. Fire Child is a part of society and is addressed by a kinship term. Because he causes the death of Ohẽy through the use of his uncontrolled power, however, he feels shame (omyk), voluntarily exiles himself from culture, and goes to live in the jungle. But culture

needs the uncontrolled power of Fire at intervals to
tame the jungle, and so he provides a means whereby,
through prescribed ritual and song, society can call
him back to serve in a limited way.

From the point of view of Ohẽy, the story contrasts his foolishness (sikirip) with the sensible
attitude of the rest of society. He goes out into a
dangerous field while the rest of the community stays
in the safety of the village. As a result, he dies and
society lives on.

This story was given to us in the heat of the dry
season, at the time for burning fields, just before
planting. My husband participated in the ritual in the
field when the song was sung to call Fire Child to
come and burn the field. This is seen as a dangerous
time. All the villagers are busy protecting children,
protecting houses to make sure their palm-thatch roofs
are not ignited and seeing that the fire does not
spread into the village. People are warned not to
visit the burnt field for a few days after the
burning.

The Karitiana believe that Fire Child still lives
in the jungle and that, in response to the song,
returns to burn the field. The Karitiana set fire to
the edges of the new field, but it is Fire Child who
burns it thoroughly. His powerful fire, which causes
death and so cannot be tolerated in the village, is
implicitly contrasted with the controlled fire in the
village, contained in hearths or cooking places and
not a danger to life.

An enemy attack

This story tells how the wife of a man
named Poren, while on a trip to her garden
to get sweet cassava, sees evidence of a
raiding party (opok `foreigner, barbarian´)
in the area. She returns home to warn her
husband, but he does not believe her. Accus-
ing her rather of meeting a lover in the
field, he becomes angry and beats her. Later
he makes a small basket which he laughingly
says will be his `head place´--the barbari-
ans will carry away his head in it.

Later, as the family sleeps, the raiding party does come. Only the wife, who had first given the warning, hears them. The barbarians break a hole into the house, push a torch through, and begin to shoot in arrows. As Poren cries out that he is being killed by the warriors, his wife reminds him that he said there were none. She runs away and escapes, but the barbarians eat Poren, his other wife, and his kinsmen. They do carry away his head in the basket he had made, and from his blood are born the opok ti oky birds (`barbarians-who-kill´ birds).

The next day his surviving kinsmen return to see what has happened and discover the birds. They find that his basket is gone and that his head has been taken, all because he did not heed his wife's warning.

In this text, we again see the geographic contrast between the village and the outside world, but the structure is best seen by examining the social relationships which exist between participants.

There are a number of contrasts between Poren (male) and his wife (female). The wife warns of danger, but he accuses of adultery. The wife heeds the warning and is wakeful, but he is unheeding and sleeps. His wife is believing and right, but he is unbelieving (kymawak) and wrong. As a result, the wife lives and he dies. Poren is inappropriately violent when he beats his wife, but she behaves appropriately throughout the story, submitting to the beating.

When we compare Poren the insider with the barbarians, he epitomizes culture, they epitomize nature. He is violent within society (the context of culture) whereas they are violent in nature. The barbarians-who-kill birds are a continuing reminder of this. The possibility of an enemy raid is an ever-present preoccupation of the Karitiana. Evidence of their activity near the village is reported many times a year, and everyone becomes very afraid, some even fleeing into the jungle for safety. At these times the men usually maintain watch at night just in case the barbarians should come.

The Karitiana maintain a clear distinction between themselves (yjja `us´) and outsiders of all
kinds (who are called opok and include other indigenous groups, Brazilians, and any other outsiders).
Anyone in the category `us´ is distinguished by an
ability to speak Karitiana and is called by a kinship
term.

The themes dealt with in this text are very
pertinent to Karitiana life. Wife-beating is common,
but is severely sanctioned. Violence is unacceptable
within the group. This is overtly expressed in the
marriage ceremony, which includes a harangue by the
parents of the couple telling the man how he should
provide for and not beat his wife. A new bride is also
told how to behave appropriately--by providing food,
for example, for her husband. She is told not to go
out at night and not to encourage the advances of
other men. This reflects a fear on the part of the men
that their wives will be tempted into illicit liai-
sons. When a wife must go to the city for medical
attention and her husband cannot accompany her, he
worries a great deal about her safety from the advances of other males.

The place for sexual relations is in the village
only. Illicit sex takes place outside the village.
Culturally acceptable sexual relations occur in the
context of marriage.

I at first thought this story was primarily about
male/female relations and, from a female point of
view, was dealing with an antipathy towards wife-
beating. While this may still be true, I now believe
the text explores the ambivalent roles of men in
Karitiana society. Within the borders of culture, they
must not behave violently; but outside culture, when
they engage in raiding and warfare, they must behave
violently--they become like foreigners (opok). The
story is thus saying that an occasional outbreak of
violence within society may be excused on two accounts: (1) there are contexts in which males are
obliged to be violent, and (2) in comparison with the
measure of violence outside the community, violence
within the community is insignificant.

There are parallels between this text and the
story of Fire Child. When uncontrolled nature is

allowed into culture, trouble ensues. Fire brings death and so do foreigners--the relation is the same.

Sexual abnormality

This text tells of a man named Okorokot who, having been rejected by the women of his village, shamelessly (ogop) makes love to a tree. He is observed by a young man who sees him making a basket which he gives to the tree as a gift. He addresses the tree as though it were a person and has sexual intercourse with a hole in the tree.

While Okorokot is making another basket, the young man decides to put pepper on the hole in the tree. He then hides and waits for Okorokot to return.

Okorokot gives the new basket to the tree, but when he penetrates the hole the pepper has its effect and he runs away to plunge into the river, to the taunts of the young man.

At last Okorokot feels shame (omyk) for what he has done and does not return to the village.

The contrasts in this story are between the unacceptable behavior of Okorokot and that of `cultured´ men and women of society. The latter represent appropriate sexuality in society, whereas Okorokot represents inappropriate sexuality in/with nature.

While reciprocity is correct in society, it is incorrect in nature, where exploitation is the norm. It is thus wrong for Okorokot to give a gift to a tree. Society punishes Okorokot for this aberrant behavior and he flees in shame.

It is important to notice that when the young man puts pepper on the tree he says, "Okorokot actually made love to a hole in a tree, so we will put pepper on it." By means of the plural pronoun the narrator indicates that the young man is acting as a representative of society in the punishment he inflicts.

Okorokot´s punishment is appropriate to Karitiana
society, which has no written legal code, no courts,
nor police authorities. Such a society punishes aberrant behavior by ostracism and shame so that the
shamed party cannot face his neighbors.

This story is a counterpoint to the two previously discussed, which have dealt with the dire conse-
quences of nature penetrating society. This story
deals with the ill-effects of society penetrating
nature in an inappropriate way. It is thus a mirror
image of the other two tales.

Ejot visits the Sky

This last tale tells of a man named
Ejot who goes to visit the sky because, when
he plants his field, the rains fail to fall
as usual and all the newly-sprouted shoots
die. As Ejot searches for a way to the sky,
he finds hunting and warfare talismans which
he collects to help him.

He eventually finds the place to climb
up to the sky, and when he ascends, he soon
finds a personage named Motỹnh, to whom he
explains his problem and sufferings. Motỹnh
then supplies him with new cuttings, and
afterwards gives him food.

Ejot and his companions are directed to
look at and lick the anus of one of the
women of the sky named Pipyt and, through
this, learn how to defecate correctly. Those
who do so are accepted by Motỹnh; those who
continue to defecate the wrong way--through
their throats--are killed.

The men are then told how to correctly
engage in sexual intercourse with Motỹnh´s
wife Tomoty. Those who follow instructions
survive; those who forget are killed. The
surviving men then return to earth and plant
the food they have received.

The two most important structural areas of this
story seem to be economic and cosmological. Cosmologically, the universe is divided into the realm of the

Karitiana (inside), the realm of hunting and killing (outside), and the realm of the sky (as opposed to down on the earth).

Economically, the lack of horticultural food at the beginning of the text is contrasted with its abundance at the end. Horticultural food is supplied by the sky; game food is supplied by nature. One must

go up to ensure a supply of vegetable food, but out to ensure a supply of animal food.

Lévi-Strauss (1955) analyzes a Pueblo myth which he suggests is dealing with tensions between agriculture and hunting. He suggests that the periodicity of agriculture implies a recurring cycle of life and death, whereas hunting involves only death. The result of agriculture is, in the end, life; but the result of hunting is death. He finds the dilemma of death to be integrated into life in agriculture. The question arises as to whether the Karitiana are exploring this same dilemma in their mythological statements concerning agriculture and hunting. Men journey to the sky because they need vegetable seed to plant, but the journey results in death for some of the party even though the need is supplied.

Cosmologically, sky and earth, the homes respectively of gods and men, contrast. Men have a need; the gods meet that need. The gods are normal in function, men are abnormal or deficient, and the gods help correct these abnormalities. In contrast to the unchanging steadiness of men, the gods are ambivalent, sometimes acting for the good of men, sometimes for their harm. The gods control agriculture and so vegetable food, but men control hunting and animal food. In the sky, there is danger for men; but on earth, among other men, there is safety. This is because on earth, in society, men retain control; but in the sky the gods are in control.

Although the story stresses differences between sky and earth, there are a few ways in which the differences are reduced. Beings in the sky, for example, are addressed by and respond with kinship terms. In this sense, they can be said to be included in society.

The behavior of both male and female sky beings is ambivalent. Motỹnh supplies needed food, but kills those who defecate incorrectly. Pipyt helps to solve this problem, but Tomoty kills those who do not observe correct sexual behavior.

Lévi-Strauss. (1955) says that it is common for mythical figures to be endowed with contradictory attributes, both good and bad. Karitiana sky beings have some attributes common to trickster figures in mythology (Pelton 1980). They are ambiguous and equivocal, halfway between two poles (Lévi-Strauss 1955). Karitiana sky gods are not quite culture, and yet not quite nature. They oscillate between the two. They are marginal to culture, yet also the originators of it in that they supply vegetable food.

The various experiences of the men who visit the sky also reflect trickster tales in their concern with bodily functions and orifices. The episodes are concerned with eating, defecation, and sexual intercourse. These things all have to do with nature, according to Lévi-Strauss. The men who previously defecated by vomiting via their throats are helped by a female sky being to defecate acceptably, and so avoid death at the hands of a male sky being. A male sky being tells them how to correctly terminate sexual intercourse to avoid death from a female sky being. Thus, even in the sky, correct behavior and correct speech save from death.

A further comment needs to be made concerning the men's sexual relations with Tomoty in this final tale. The men are told not to indicate to the woman when they have completed her impregnation. If they do, she has no further need of them and kills them. Men must keep this to themselves to avoid giving women the power of death. Male/female rivalry is here explored, but the solution is that both men and women are needed for culture to endure. Sexual relations in culture are not limited to impregnation; ongoing social relationships are required as well.

The sky, then, is where communitas reigns (Bastien 1983). It is there that distinctions are neutralized and both creative and disruptive forces reign. The sky world of the Karitiana is the expression of communitas which helps humanitas to continue. The control men maintain on earth is not valid in the sky.

Man must relinquish control to the sky beings and is at their mercy. As Pelton (1980) states, each society needs communitas and the creative tensions it embodies. In suspending the values and law and order of culture in one sphere (the sky), their potency is reinforced in another (on earth, in society). Through contact with the sky, order is promulgated, new patterns are set up, and norms are established. An economic problem is solved through provision of food plants; a physical problem is solved when men learn how to defecate properly; and sexual rivalry is resolved when men learn how to have correct sexual relationships.

But how does the above analysis correspond with Karitiana daily life? In real life, the Karitiana appear to take vegetable food for granted because it is usually in good supply. Crops rarely fail. Their main preoccupation is with the meat supply. When a person complains of being hungry, he means he has had no meat. This reflects a short-term lack of control over the supply of game. No man can be sure when he goes hunting that he will not return empty-handed.

The concern with control over society and the environment is also reflected in other aspects of Karitiana life. Until recently, the Karitiana constituted small bands leading a precarious existence in a hostile environment. Their hold upon culture was tenuous, and it is not surprising that their mythology expresses a concern with maintaining control over sexuality, aberrant behavior, and other threats to society. Accounts of occasional episodes of gang rape in recent genealogical history are evidence enough that the gulf between culture and chaos is not wide. The danger of a cultural breakdown is real, and an emphasis upon control is understandable.

NOTE

[1]The Karitiana constitute a single community of some 75 persons located 100km from the city of Porto Velho in the State of Rondônia, Brazil. Karitiana belongs to the Arikem branch of the Tupí family of languages. The data for this paper were gathered as part of a long-range project of the Summer Institute of Linguistics through contracts with the Ministry of the Interior, the National Indian Foundation (FUNAI),

and the National Museum, Rio de Janeiro. The author
expresses her appreciation to her husband, David, for
his participation with her in this research.

REFERENCES

Bastien, Joseph W. 1979. Mountain of the condor: meta-
    phor and ritual in an Andean ayllu. American
    Ethnology Society monograph 64.

Carroll, Michael P. 1981. Lévi-Strauss, Freud and the
    Trickster: a new perspective upon an old problem.
    American ethnologist 8:301-13.

Leach, Edmund. 1970. Lévi-Strauss. London: Wm. Collins
    & Co.

Lévi-Strauss, Claude. 1955. The structural study of
    myth. Journal of American folklore 68:428-44.

------. 1966. The savage mind. Chicago: University of
    Chicago Press.

------. 1967. The story of Asdiwal. In Leach (ed.),
    The structural study of myth and totemism, pp. 1-
    74. (=Association of Social Anthropologists Mono-
    graph 5). London: Tavistock Publications.

------. 1969. The raw and the cooked, introduction to a
    science of mythology: 1. New York: Harper and
    Row.

Pelton, Robert D. 1980. The trickster in West Africa:
    a study of mythic irony and sacred delight.
    Berkeley: University of California Press.

Yalman, Nur. 1967. The raw : the cooked :: nature :
    culture--observations on Le cru et le cuit. In
    Edmund Leach (ed.), The structural study of myth
    and totemism, pp. 91-99 (=Association of Social
    Anthropologists Monograph 5). London: Tavistock
    Publications.

PROBLEMS IN PAUMARI ACCULTURATION

Shirley Chapman

Summer Institute of Linguistics, Brazil

Because of an understandable desire to retain
traditional behavioral patterns and values, the Paumarí have failed to adopt new economic patterns which
might be expected to meet current felt needs (Goodenough 1963:37). This introductory study of Paumarí[1]
acculturation indicates that for economic innovations
to be acceptable to the Paumarí they will need to take
into account, in particular, the nomadic character of
their traditional way of life.

As of 1974, the Paumarí had failed to accept net
fishing, lumber cutting, and rubber tapping from Portuguese-speaking neighbors (hereinafter referred to as
`outsiders´) because such activities clash with tradi-
tional ones.

Although net fishing would appear to meet the
felt need of the Paumarí for an increased food supply,
this occupation had not been adopted extensively by
the Paumarí. They preferred traditional fishing patterns of using traps and arrows. When metal was
brought in, they adopted harpoons and fishhooks, but
this did not interfere with the pattern of daily
fishing to provide for immediate needs. No process of
fish preservation needed to be learned or exercised,
and a nomadic way of life was preserved.

The Paumarí traditionally keep little or no supply of food on hand for days when they are unable to
fish. They frequently have no food left over from one
day to the next. When it rains and they cannot fish,
they frequently go hungry. When most of the men go on
a fishing trip for outsiders, the women are often left
behind without food. They can usually fend for them-

71

selves if they have a canoe and fishhooks. The Paumarí keep only a very small quantity of items such as cassava meal, salt, matches, and kerosene, items which require repeated trips to purchase from outsiders. A man who catches a large fish will often have to go and buy the salt needed to preserve it. A second trip is then made to sell the salted fish.

Due to the expense involved, long fish nets require joint ownership. This clashes with the Paumarí idea of individual ownership. An object is always owned by a particular Paumarí and joint ownership is rare. Possessions are individually owned, even between a husband and wife. An article is owned by the person who made or bought it unless it was made for another. Parents often designate a portion of their field as belonging to a particular child even if the child is not old enough to appreciate or benefit from such a gift.

Lumber cutting has not been accepted by the Paumarí because it is so time consuming. It interferes with traditional fishing patterns still in use as the most direct means of obtaining food. Rubber tapping is an unpopular occupation for the same reason. Its close association with labor to clear debts is an added drawback. Little enthusiasm is shown for working to pay for merchandise already expended, and there is no clear cut concept of debt as western culture defines that term.

Attempts to meet felt needs

Even so, changes have already been made by the Paumarí to meet some of their felt needs. These changes, although not adequate for solving all their problems, are a step towards improving their economic situation.

Through Planting

The Paumarí have accepted the idea of planting crops on nonflood ground, even though this is a departure from traditional practice. This has by no means replaced the older practice of beach planting and nomadic wandering, but it may well be a factor that could lead to economic improvement in a more settled way of life.

Planting on high ground is an attempt to overcome
a shortage of cassava meal. This has entailed the need
for poison from the outside to control leaf-cutter
ants. Livestock and some new crops such as corn and
beans have also been incorporated to a limited degree.
The Paumarí are just now beginning to experiment with
rice.

The Paumarí continue to plant on some of the
sandy beaches along the river. Such planting is relatively easy. The level of the rivers changes by
approximately forty feet. As the waters gradually
subside and the ground dries a little, the heavy
grassy weeds are cut down and crops planted. The
growing season is quite short so planting starts as
soon as possible, from May to July. The sandy beaches
yield a better crop in shorter time than high ground
which does not flood.

In the past, horticulture played only a small
part in Paumarí economy. Now the difficulty and cost
of buying meal causes the Paumarí to plant their own
cassava. Cassava planted on sandy beaches must be
harvested before the rising river reaches it, from
November to February, lest it rot.

On high ground, a slash-and-burn type of horticulture is employed. Such fields involve heavy work in
clearing the forest of large trees as well as smaller
undergrowth. Clearing starts as the rainy season ends.
Bitter cassava is the main crop, supplemented by sweet
cassava, squash, corn, and several varieties of yam.
The cassava can remain in the ground for two years
before it must be harvested; but because of a chronic
shortage of cassava meal, the Paumarí tend to harvest
the roots when very small, thereby losing some of the
reward of their labor.

Although the Paumarí are planting more than in
the past, they primarily remain fishermen, and not
farmers. They have a desire to plant enough so that
they will not have to buy cassava meal, but none has
yet reached that goal. If a Brazilian invites the men
to go on a fishing trip and promises attractive payment in merchandise or drink, they usually go, even
though it may be just the time when they should be
planting.

Through the production of artifacts

Paumarí women have increased their production of woven goods for sale to outsiders to satisfy their desire for products from the outside. They are able to do this, improving their economic position to some degree, without interference with their nomadic pattern. The market for such woven goods is not constant, however, so that this does not provide the women with regular income.

The production of artifacts is also an acceptable activity for men and may prove to be a factor in moving towards a more stable economic situation.

Through education

Some Paumarí recognize the need for a knowledge of elementary arithmetic in order to adequately handle commercial transactions. Although the provision of such skills requires the development of new educational institutions, it would significantly change their present understanding of how to handle finances, providing a greater understanding of how to compete within the framework of the Brazilian economic system.

The Paumarí continue to teach their children the traditional skills needed for adult life. Fathers teach their sons how to fish and hunt. Mothers teach their daughters how to cook and weave. Learning is primarily through observation and apprenticeship; there is no formal teaching.

The Paumarí have learned some new skills from outsiders. Women have learned to cut and sew clothing for themselves and their families. Men have learned to make wooden canoes and the same type of paddle as outsiders use. They have also learned how to make cassava meal. These skills have been acquired by helping and observing the Portuguese-speaking Brazilians.

More recently, the Paumarí have been given the opportunity to learn how to read and write. Such study fits no previous pattern of activity, the teachers of necessity in the beginning not being their parents and requiring formal instruction. Quite a few Paumarí have, nevertheless, shown a real desire to master the elements of arithmetic and to become literate. Their

motivation seems to be a desire to send written com-
munications and to avoid being cheated in commercial
transactions. Some have taken advantage of such training offered by members of the Summer Institute of
Linguistics, but others show no real interest in education of this type.

Not all who enthusiastically began to attend
reading classes have continued them. Fishing, planting, and the desire to move from place to place
accounts for many dropouts. Of eleven women who completed a first unit of study, five continued on and
are now able, with limited ability, to read and write
in Portuguese as well as in their own language. Women
tend to have more time to acquire such skills, both in
and out of class, since they are at home more than the
men.

As of 1974, reading classes have remained an
extracurricular activity and not a part of the regular
Paumarí life style. A few men follow an erratic schedule of asking for individual classes on their own.
Others have said they would like to learn, but have
never begun to attend classes. The daily quest for
food and material goods is given a higher priority
than their desire for formal education.

Commercial dealings and authority structures

Commercial dealings with outsiders entail relationships and authority structures which are alien to
Paumarí customary patterns of sharing. Although the
Paumarí do not have a pattern of strong individual
leadership from the past, there now appears to be a
need for a neutral party to mediate both in contacts
with outsiders and between themselves.

Among themselves, each man works for himself and
his family. On jobs that require extra manpower, such
as in making a field, opening a canoe, or roofing a
house, he either uses a reciprocal work system or
makes payment with food or some suitable gift. When a
woman sews for her wifeless relative, some gift is
given in exchange. Similarly, the service of a midwife
or shaman is paid by a gift. Such payment seems to be
a token exchange rather than relating directly to the
value of the service performed.

Employer relationships and sharing patterns

The employer-employee relationship which the Paumarí have come to accept with outsiders is foreign to their traditional way of life. Their traditional system of sharing included the sharing of time and energy as well as food and other material artifacts. Helping one another accrued to the benefit of all. In the Paumarí language, they `work´ for outsiders but `help´ one another.

Two words are used to express the idea of helping. One word means to help someone do a job he is already involved in, such as preparing a field for planting. The other word means to help a person who is unable to help himself. Only a shaman, for example, can extract a sickness seed from a sick person. Neither of these words are used in reference to work for an outsider, where the Paumari have come to expect a time and energy correlation between work done and remuneration received.

In the past, money was associated with the acquisition of merchandise and was never necessary for obtaining food. An abundant supply of fish in the past and the traditional system of sharing insured an adequate daily food supply. Even today, there is a reluctance to use money to buy food, apart from cassava meal, indicating that the concept of working for money to buy food has not been widely accepted.

NOTE

[1]This paper is based on fieldwork carried out in Brazil under the auspices of the Summer Institute of Linguistics during the period from 1964 to 1974, under contracts with the Ministry of the Interior, the National Indian Foundation (FUNAI), and the National Museum, Rio de Janeiro. The Paumarí people number around 250. The data represented in this paper are restricted to a group of about 160 persons who live in the area of São Clemente of the Purus River in the State of Amazonas. The Paumarí language is classified as Arawakan (Metraux, 1948:667).

The paper was written at a workshop held in Pôrto Velho, State of Rondônia, during November and December of 1974, and represents the Paumarí situation of that time. A number of significant changes have taken place in the intervening ten years which deserve further research. The writer wishes to express her thanks to Margaret Sheffler for her guidance and for many helpful suggestions concerning the organization and presentation of the material.

REFERENCES

Goodenough, Ward Hunt. 1963. Cooperation in Change. New York: Russell Sage Foundation.

Metraux, Alfred. 1948. Tribes of the Western Amazon Basin: Tribes of the Jurua-Purus Basins. Handbook of South American Indians 4. Washington, D.C.: Smithsonian Institution.

URUBU-KAAPOR GIRLS' PUBERTY RITES

Kiyoko Kakumasu

Summer Institute of Linguistics, Brazil

When there is a sudden change of behavior associated with physiological changes, such as at weaning
or at adolescence, there is a state of discontinuity.
Management of discontinuity often involves special
rites and ceremonies. During the initiation ceremonies
for adolescence, there is often an acceleration of
teaching and learning. This, in turn, produces good,
well-informed citizens who maintain the cultural
heritage.

This paper attempts to show that Urubu-Kaapor[1]
girls' puberty rites, with changes over the years,
continue to meet contemporary needs. In order to show
these changes, a comparison of Urubu-Kaapor rites is
made with Tupinambá[2] girls' rites and attention is
called to some of the events and factors which have
contributed to change. Various needs that are met by
the continued observation of the rites are also discussed. Tupinambá rites are recounted first in order
to provide an historical framework since it is likely
that Tupinambá rites constitute a link to the proto
rites. Van Gennep's (1960) taxonomy is employed in the
analysis of both Urubu-Kaapor and Tupinambá rites.

The van Gennep Taxonomy

Societies employ various means to indicate the
advancement of their members through various stages of
life. Rituals which accompany this advancement from
stage to stage are termed 'rites of passage' by van
Gennep (1960:2f). Through the analysis of various
examples of such rituals, van Gennep found a different
type of rite for each of three different rites of
passage.

He maintains that, in Rites of Separation, a novice is mutilated in some way to symbolize removal from the common mass of humanity. This is the function of circumcision, tooth pulling, cutting of the little finger above the last joint, tattooing, or cutting the hair in a particular fashion. With the exception of hair cutting, such operations leave ineradicable traces, making incorporation into a defined group permanent.

During Rites of Transition, various types of instruction are given to prepare an initiate for a new role. Orientation to secret lore and moral instruction, including proper sexual behavior, may be given. Dietary taboos are often observed during this phase of the ceremony.

In Rites of Incorporation, an initiate presents or shares food with another individual or group. Van Gennep further suggests, for example, that at the time of her first menstruation, a female initiate enters a new status and becomes `sacred´ to others who remain in a profane state. "This new condition calls for rites and eventually for reincorporating the individual into the group and returning him [or her] to the customary routines of life" (1960:ix). These three types are not developed to the same extent by all peoples or in every ceremonial pattern.

In his classic study of cultural celebrations, van Gennep "accepted the dichotomy of the sacred and profane; in fact, this is a central concept for understanding his transitional stage in which [he feels] an individual or group finds itself from time to time," according to Solon Kimball (van Gennep 1960:ix). The sacred is not an absolute value, but one relative to the situation. The person who enters a status at variance with the one he previously held becomes `sacred´ to the others who remain in the profane state. It is this new condition which calls for rites eventually incorporating the individual into the group and returning him to the customary routines of life ready to fulfill his new role. Without the recognized rituals these changes could be dangerous or, at least, upsetting to the life of the group and the individual. Rites of passage, then, help cushion the disturbance during the transitional period.

Rites of passage generally mark at least four primary crises within the life cycle. These are birth, transition from childhood to adulthood or puberty, transition from the unmarried state to the married, and the transition from life to death. It is the transition from childhood to adulthood for females that will be the focus of this paper.

For most societies the sign indicating that a girl has reached puberty is the beginning of menstruation. Unlike male rites, therefore, female puberty rites tend to occur spontaneously and with little advance preparation.

The menstruous girl may be viewed culturally as either `unclean` or `blessed`. Among the Urubu-Kaapor, a man becomes unlucky (panem) in hunting if, even unknowingly, he sleeps with a menstruous woman (Huxley 1963:145). Among the Pueblo people of the Southwestern United States, however, such a girl is regarded as a source of rich spiritual blessing, and in some elaborate religious ceremonies these girls may bless the priests by virtue of their condition (Nida 1954:115). The rites of passage of a particular society generally show an inclination toward one of these two viewpoints.

Tupinambá Girls' Puberty Rites

Perhaps the earliest documentation of the Tupinambá girls' puberty rites is that chronicled by André Thevet. According to Thevet (1575:946f), the first menstruation was called quioundu-ar. The Tupinambá celebrated it with drunkenness. A young girl had great fear of this first menstruation because the initiation rites could be very painful. The hair on her head was cut off with a fish tooth (which, Thevet said, cuts very well), as close to the head as possible. The few hairs that were left were singed off. The girl was then placed in a standing position on a flat stone where the Tupinambá used to make necklaces.

There, those conducting the rites scratched the skin of the girl's back in the form of a cross, with the tooth of an animal, from the shoulders to the buttocks. Some girls were scratched more deeply than others, depending upon how much pain and bleeding they could withstand. After that, ashes made from a wild

squash were rubbed into the wound. The ashes caused
pain and left a permanent scar. It was said that if
the girl was not cut in this manner, her abdomen would
not do well and her children would be malformed.

Then her arms were tied to her body with cotton
string and capybara teeth were strung around her neck.
This was done so that her own teeth would grow stronger and thus she could chew the cassava tuber used in
making the drink called kaouin. After that, she had to
lie down in an old hammock and was not allowed out of
it until three days had passed.

During these three days she was completely covered so that no one could see her, and she fasted--no
eating or drinking. If she needed to relieve herself,
her mother, aunt, or grandmother carried her, taking
along a red-hot piece of charcoal in a clay vessel and
a bit of cotton thread to ward off any evil spirit (?)
known as Mae which might otherwise come close or even
enter her genitals.

After three days had passed, the girl got out of
her hammock, stepping down onto the same flat stone
used in her initiation, so that she would not touch
the ground with her feet. She was then given cassava
meal (farinha) to eat and roots cooked without salt or
meat. She was not permitted to drink anything but
water. It appears that this was her diet for the first
month.

During her menstrual flow, a girl cleaned herself
with a stick about three feet long. She remained
inactive in her hammock until the beginning of her
second menstruation, which usually took about a month.

At the time of the second menstruation, the girl
had incisions made on her chest and abdomen, as well
as new incisions on her back. Dietary restrictions
were not as severe as during the first month, but she
was still not permitted to talk to anyone. Neither was
she permitted to go to the gardens nor to do any of
the things she had been able to do prior to menstruation. She remained in her hammock and spun cotton.

In the third month, after having been painted all
black with the juice of the genipa fruit, a girl was
permitted to go to the gardens again. The Tupinambá
believed that if she did not observe these rules, the

spirit Mermona[3] would cause everyone to die (Thevet 1575:946f).

It appears that the Tupinambá focused a great deal of attention upon the teaching of adult skills during puberty rites. Montoya (1879, according to Fernandes 1963:272f) says that an initiate was sent to an adult woman who made her work to the point of exhaustion. Errors were penalized with severe punishment and the girl had to acquire skills needed for homemaking.

When a girl's hair had grown again to shoulder length, she was considered marriageable.

Métraux (1950:204) suggests that the reason for the painful ordeal suffered by young girls was to shelter them from danger that threatens them at this critical period of development. Fernandes (1963:273) noted that the initiation of women among the Tupinambá implied the observance of rites of death and of rebirth. It is likely that both of these aspects entered into Tupinambá thinking.

There was a striking similarity between Tupinambá practices when someone dies and the treatment of a pubescent girl at her first menstruation. A pubescent girl, for example, covered herself in a hammock and did not eat for the first three days of the first month. She was considered and treated as though she were dead, in that she was carried by her female relatives whenever she needed to relieve herself. This activity also went on during what van Gennep calls Rites of Transition.

Analysis according to van Gennep. I suggest that the hair cutting and the scratching belong to a Rite of Separation as defined by van Gennep. Tying a girl's arms to her body with a string, tying capybara teeth around her neck, seclusion and fasting for three days, being carried out to relieve herself--all these were part of the Rite of Separation which began with hair cutting and ended with her breaking her fast.

I interpret the restricted diet, the cotton spinning which could require instruction, and orientation to beliefs regarding the initiation rites themselves as constituting a Rite of Transition according to van Gennep's scheme.

Additional incisions on other parts of the body, continued abstinence from talking and from any activity previously engaged in--such as going to the gardens--were some of the other activities included during this second stage which began with her breaking her fast and ended with scarification of other parts of her body.

Van Gennep's suggestion concerning the presentation of food or the sharing of a meal as a Rite of Incorporation are not present in the document which concerns Tupinambá rites.

I suggest that when the initiate paints herself with the genipa fruit paint and begins to return to the gardens, it is at this point that she is incorporated into the adult community, since it is a return to a normal activity of an Urubu-Kaapor adult.

Urubu-Kaapor Girls' Puberty Rites

Among the Urubu-Kaapor people, menstruation is called jai (Kakumasu 1968). At her first menstruation, the pubescent girl enters a palm-leaf enclosed room, called kapyk, for a period of isolation. This enclosure is made in the sleeping area of the home. It is the same type of enclosure used for the isolation of parents of a new-born baby.

The girl sleeps alone in a hammock in this enclosure for a month. "Her feet [are] kept clear of the ground, lest the magic that [is] in her should escape in a kind of short circuit" (Huxley 1963:155). She bathes with warm water that her mother heats for her. During her seclusion "the girl spins a long carauá string to distribute to her relatives, part of which serves as the attachment of her feather necklace which she wears when she abandons her place of seclusion" (Ribeiro and Ribeiro 1957:148).

On the seventh day of isolation, her father cuts her hair as short as possible, using a pair of scissors. Studies by others on hair cutting reveal that it is often seen as a means of ridding a person of a dangerous state, to end a taboo, or to purify oneself of the influence of death or the ghost to which a person had been exposed (Fraser 1922:258-87).

Food is given to her from the beginning of menstruation, but the diet is strictly limited. She eats only cooked white cassava meal (u´i) and stewed white tortoise (jaxi te) until the hair on her head grows out again a bit. Then her legs are scratched with the tooth of an agouti, and a white string is tied around her neck with bows tied in front and back with the same string.

Cloth binders are wrapped around the stomach and forehead, and the girl´s father puts large ants (tapia´ɨ) into the binders. After she has suffered some painful bites, the binders are removed. In a culture where it is desirable and admirable for a person to be strong (pyratã), the girl is not supposed to cry audibly. The Urubu-Kaapor explain that pain is inflicted to make her strong.

Huxley (1963:148f) suggests that this is done to atone for her guilt feelings. When she menstruates for the first time, she is repeating woman´s age-old offence of contradicting man´s pretensions, showing that it is she who makes children, not man. This is her guilt, and by this the contradiction of the masculine world of mythology and the feminine world of physical reality is resolved. The mythological contention is that the creation of human life is an exclusive function of the male. This is contested by the life-producing menstruation; hence, a sense of guilt results.

Food taboos are maintained from the beginning of menstruation for several months, at which time the girl is ready for marriage. After the hair on her head grows a little, a larger, orange-spotted tortoise (Port. carumbé) is added to her diet. Certain fishes (jandi´a and karaiwa) are also added. In the sixth month, when her hair has grown long, she begins to eat deer, tapir, the small wild pig, and agouti. In the eighth month, she adds the large wild pig (Port. queixada). The reason given for abstinence from all but tortoise meat in the early stages of first menstruation is that a girl would otherwise go crazy and die.

A month after her first menstruation, when the initiate comes out of isolation, her father peels some cassava for her and she begins to perform the toasting process. She makes balls of soft cassava and places

them in the sun to bleach. She cuts and gathers firewood for the fire and toasts the cassava grains by
herself. When the toasting is done, she shares some of
the grains with each major household of the village.
She then grates other cassava tubers, boils the mass,
and makes sweet unfermented drink for her family.

After she has completed all this--her seclusion,
the toasting of cassava, and the preparation of the
cassava drink--she begins to wear the adult woman's
feather necklace. She also begins to wear the woman's
waistband, sewn for her by her mother of Job's tears
(Lat. Coix lacryma-jobi). At the end of the waistband
are hung feathered flowers. This is worn over an
everyday denim skirt. The girl applies pink lipstick
plant paint (Port. uruku) to her face in horizontal
lines between her eyebrows and on her chin, and in a
vertical line on her cheeks. This facial application
of fruit paint is for both ceremonial and casual
cosmetics. The young woman emerges into adulthood with
the assurance of her competence to fulfill her future
obligations and impressed with the importance of her
role.

Analysis according to van Gennep. The hair cutting of the Urubu-Kaapor initiate may be considered,
in van Gennep's view, as being a Rite of Separation.
Isolation, warm-water baths, scratching of legs and
the tying of string around the neck are activities
which occur during this rite, which begins with the
hair cutting and ends with the string tying.

The dietary taboo, cotton spinning with accom-
panying instruction in beliefs about rites and sexual
privileges are the activities I consider to belong to
the Rites of Transition, according to van Gennep's
frame of reference. Endurance of the ant bites on
stomach and forehead is practiced during this period,
which begins with dietary taboos and ends with spinning and instruction.

For the Rites of Incorporation, the presentation
of cassava grains to the village and the sharing of
sweet cassava drink with her family are central. This
rite begins with the gathering of firewood and the
toasting of cassava and ends with her adornment in
ceremonial wear of the adult woman.

Comparison of Tupinambá and Urubu-Kaapor Rites

In the Tupinambá Rite of Separation, scarification by scratching and rubbing with ashes was practiced to assure normal offspring for the initiate. Incisions in chest, abdomen, and back and hair-cutting were also practiced.

In the Urubu-Kaapor rite, scratching of the initiate's legs to the point of bleeding is practiced, but no scar-producing agent is used. There is no repetition of scratching nor does there seem to be a belief like that of the Tupinambá concerning mutilation.

The modern use of scissors for hair-cutting makes singeing unnecessary. Other Tupinambá activities not practiced by the Urubu-Kaapor are: tying of the initiate's arms to her body and the initial three-day fast. The metaphor of death as a part of the Rite of Separation appears to be weakened. Urubu-Kaapor substitutions are: the tying of string around the neck instead of capybara teeth, seclusion in a room for a month instead of being covered in a hammock for three days, warm baths instead of the use of a cleaning stick, and an amplified diet.

In the Tupinambá Rite of Transition, very restrictive dietary taboos were enforced throughout two full months of seclusion. Cotton spinning was possibly accompanied by instruction in ritual beliefs.

The Urubus-Kaapores have omitted the fast during the first three days of first menstruation. A restricted diet from the first day is augmented in succeeding weeks and months. The purpose of abstinence from certain game is taught. Cotton spinning is common to both groups. Orientation to acceptable sexual behavior takes place during this period. The Urubus-Kaapores add an endurance test, using biting ants, that is lacking among the Tupinambá.

The Tupinambá Rite of Incorporation into adult society began with the initiate returning to the gardens and to other menial tasks in the third month of menstruation. The Urubu-Kaapor initiate shares toasted cassava grains with each major household of her village and shares sweet cassava drink with her family at the end of just one month. The Urubu-Kaapor initiate

then dons the ceremonial dress which marks her entrance into adulthood, this being shown for the Tupinambá initiate by permanent scars.

Changes in Environment and in Rites

Leighton made the following observation:

> Forces moving toward change, actual and
> potential, exist in all societies throughout
> the world. Sometimes these are triggered by
> aid programs, more often now they are well
> under way when the aid programs are intro-
> duced. In either case, these forces are the
> means for driving development; yet instead
> of being harnessed to this end by the inno-
> vators, they are frequently resisted and
> fought with. Because they seem overwhelming
> and disorderly, they are held back; and from
> holding back, it's a short step to blocking
> at every turn. The flood then swells and
> instead of turning the wheel bursts the dam
> and sweeps wheel, mill and all away. (Goode-
> nough 1963:7f)

This helps to explain the acceptance of modern
tools but the maintenance of distance from and a
certain degree of resistance to the outsider and his
ways that has continued among the Urubu-Kaapor people
over the years of intermittent contact with outside
forces.

In an historical overview, I would like to suggest possible reasons for the changes that occurred in
Urubu-Kaapor girls' puberty rites. Service (1962:113)
describes environment as having two aspects: (1) the
natural (organic and inorganic) environment and (2)
the presence of competing societies, the superorganic
environment. The presence and influence of the Portuguese in Brazil constituted the competing or dominat-
ing society in the life of the Urubu-Kaapor people,
and has been a powerful contributing factor toward
change in Urubu-Kaapor rites.

When the Portuguese stopped the Tupinambá from
waging wars with their neighbors, the ritual execution
of enemies stopped. Change was inevitable. Historically, interethnic wars were very much a way of life

for the Tupinambá. Young warriors were not considered men nor could they marry until they had killed an enemy. This killing took place at ceremonies. The warrior was then scratched and a permanent scar was left on his body as a sign of his membership in adult male society. Although scarification was also a part of Tupinambá girls' rites, it is not a part of the comparable Urubu-Kaapor practice of today. Without the male counterpart, the practice may have lost its significance for the Urubu-Kaapor.

The warrior also had to endure ant bites on his forehead and waist for an entire day. Although the Tupinambá rites for girls did not apparently include a similar ordeal, the Urubu-Kaapor rites still do. This may represent an innovation by the Urubu-Kaapor, along with the eating of white tortoise from the first day of menstruation.

Other likely reasons for change in Urubu-Kaapor rites are the formation of the Servico de Protecão aos Indios (SPI) in 1910 and the `pacification' of the Urubus-Kaapores in 1928. Increased contact between the Portuguese-speaking community and the Urubus-Kaapores resulted with the establishment of SPI trading posts. The education of the children of SPI personnel was started at the posts along with material goods. The introduction of perforated copper plates made the grating of cassava easier. Having strong teeth to chew cassava was no longer as important for initiates in the girls' puberty rites. The introduction of firearms by SPI personnel made the capybara scarce after a time. The reduction in population of this rodent very likely influenced the disuse of its teeth in the initiate's necklace.

Decrease in human population constitutes another reason for change in rites. Increased contact with the dominant society has resulted in the introduction of the common cold and other communicable diseases among the Urubus-Kaapores. Their practice of bathing in the cold streams to ward off fever has resulted in pneumonia and death for many. Lack of immunization or adequate medical attention has also contributed to their misery.

A resulting decrease in population may have contributed to a shortening in duration of the rites. With fewer villagers to provide tortoise meat for an

initiate, this special diet has become problematic.
The girls themselves are needed even more for subsistence activities as the population has dwindled. The
period of learning homemaking skills has been omitted
from present-day rites. Girls are no longer sent to
other women for the purpose of learning these skills.
Mothers teach them to their daughters before puberty.
The rites merely provide reinforcement of earlier
learning.

The introduction of a bartering economy at SPI
posts has also contributed to change. Contact with the
dominant society since pacification has instilled in
the Urubus-Kaapores a desire to be clothed. Men now
wear shorts, trousers, and shirts; women wear dresses.
This desire has necessitated having these items sewn
by seamstresses at the post. Payment for sewing is
made in the form of three or four tortoises per item.
The tortoise was also used, for a time, in bartering
for certain articles of cloth, tobacco, and soap. I
believe this increase in demand for tortoise, along
with the decrease in population, has influenced the
shortening in duration of the rites. It very likely
also influenced how soon other meats could be added to
the initiate's diet.

The Present-day Function of Puberty Rites

Although the Urubus-Kaapores have made changes in
their girls' puberty rites to adjust to a changing
environment, they have retained the practice because
it continues to meet present-day needs. The specific
needs of separation, instruction, and incorporation
are met through the retention of some aspects of
earlier (Tupinambá) forms, with certain additions.

The need to communicate certain facts in symbolic
mode is met: the initiate celebrates the attainment of
sexual maturity, hence the possibility of maternity;
the initiate also celebrates social maturity with its
associated responsibilities and privileges. Richards
(Firth 1975:182) says that "with a female there is
additional complication: the onset of her menstrual
flow is linked with emotionally tinged ideas about the
power of blood--negatively associated with danger and
mystical damage; and positively with creative fer-
tility. So linked with rites of protection and

purification are also those of promotion of child-bearing and domestic efficiency."

The instruction that is accomplished during the rites and post-puberty orientation is one of the most effective ways to transmit culture. The value system of the society and its justification and much of the cultural heritage of the community are taught or reinforced at this time. In quoting Hart (1955), Spindler (1974:342) says that "standardization of experience--uniformity of training is markedly present in post-initiation experience." He maintains that whereas childhood experience is part of the secular world, postpuberty experience is part of the sacred world. It is no wonder that uniformity of training is desired.

Spindler suggests that primitive societies, despite their marginal subsistence and the fact that they are frequently close to the starvation point, devote more care and attention to the production of good citizens than to the production of good technicians, and therefore they can be said to value good citizenship more highly than they value the production of good food producers. He says that this relative lack of interest in standardizing subsistence-training while insisting at the same time on standardizing training in the ideological aspects of culture, may go a long way toward enabling us to explain the old sociological problem called cultural lag. Change in technology is easier to achieve and takes place with less resistance than change in the nontechnological or ideological fields (Spindler 1974:358).

Another need being met by the continuance of puberty rites is that of group identity. In their rites, the Urubus-Kaapores maintain their identity as `dwellers of the wood´, as they like to call themselves. In spite of enduring contact with the dominant society, they have embraced little of the ideology of the outside world, though they have accepted material goods and technology. They have retained their own language and have remained, for the most part, monolingual. About 90% of the population speaks only Urubu-Kaapor. Loewen (1968:8-15) attributes cultural vitality, a functional `reason-to-be´, as one reason for the retention of a minority language. Other reasons are a relatively balanced cultural integration and the capacity to function meaningfully under contact conditions.

The Urubus-Kaapores maintain a geographic distance from trading posts. This geographic distance serves as a resistance factor to reduce the influence of the national language and culture upon the community. Service (1968:8) puts it this way: "There have been survivals into the present of ancient cultural forms which because of relative isolation have maintained stable adaptation."

Concluding Remarks

Changes have been made in Urubu-Kaapor girls' puberty rites over the years, but they continue to meet contemporary needs. They safeguard the initiate during a dangerous period of her life by separating her, by focusing supernatural power on the task of insuring her a productive life through food taboos, orientation to ritual beliefs, and by incorporating her into adult society. Celebration of her attainment to maturity is communicated symbolically through ritual. The need for ethnic identity is met. Post-puberty instruction effectively transmits cultural values and knowledge and standardizes experience leading to a uniformity of training in a society which considers it important to produce good citizens and good communicators of their cultural heritage.

Changing circumstances can lead to changes in rites either by omission or addition, depending upon whether there is a continuing function for the rites or an emphasis is needed for particular beliefs or values. Examples are the discontinuance of the use of capybara teeth around the neck of the initiate after the introduction of perforated copper plates made their use obsolete, and the addition of ant bites to emphasize endurance.

A minor socioeconomic implication also surfaces within the Urubu-Kaapor folk society today with the continuance of these rites. The heavy use of tortoise in these rites spells danger of an eventual shortage in the future. Its continued use in the period after childbirth and in bartering for kerosene in more recent years also contribute to this danger. The demarcation of the area in which these people live also contributes to this danger. Not only is there danger of a shortage of tortoise as a food supply, but of a shortage for ritual dietary needs. The time seems

opportune for the introduction of conservation prin-
ciples or of a production project.

The analysis of ritual is enhanced by comparison
with practices of the past or of the present. Comparison helps us to put our findings in perspective and to
reach a greater understanding of what we have seen.
This study analyzed the contemporary Urubu-Kaapor
girls' puberty rites, comparing them with earlier
Tupinambá practices. Van Gennep's analysis of the
function of puberty rites was used as a basis for
discussion.

NOTES

[1]Urubu-Kaapor belongs to the Tupí-Guaraní language family. There have been approximately 500 speak-
ers of this language for the past twenty-five years.
They live in the State of Maranhão, Brazil, on the
tributaries that flow into the Gurupí, Maracacume, and
Turiacu Rivers. Data for this study were gathered
during field trips to the village of Xãtarixã during
the years 1964-67, under the auspices of the Summer
Institute of Linguistics and the Museu Nacional of Rio
de Janeiro. Grateful acknowledgment is due the Servico
de Protecão aos Indios for granting authorization for
the field trips, to Barbara Moore for valuable coun-
sel, and to Fredi Tobler for translating sections of
Thevet (1575) for my use.

[2]During the 16th and 17th centuries, the Tupinambá were settled along the eastern coast of Brazil as
far north as Pará and as far south as Rio de Janeiro.

[3]Clastres (1978) refers to Thevet's mention of a
creator spirit named Monan. She also discusses the
death of a person named Maira-Monan. Maira is the
Urubu-Kaapor culture hero. My hypothesis is that the
name Mermona may be a corruption of the name Maira-
Monan.

REFERENCES

Clastres, Hèléne. 1978. Terra sem mal. Tr. by Renato
    Janine Ribeiro. São Paulo: Editora Brasiliense.

Fernandes, Florestan. 1963. Organizacão social dos
    Tupinambá. São Paulo: Difusão Européia do Livro.

Firth, Raymond. 1975. Symbols: public and private. London: George Allen and Unwin Ltd.

Fraser, James George. 1922. The Golden Bough. New York: The MacMillan Company.

Gennep, Arnold van. 1960. The rites of passage. Chicago: The University of Chicago Press.

Goodenough, Ward Hunt. 1963. Cooperation in change. New York: Russell Sage Foundation.

Hart, C. W. M. 1955. Education and anthropology. Palo Alto: Stanford University Press.

Huxley, Francis. 1963. Affable savages. London: Rupert Hart-Davis.

Kakumasu, James Y. 1968. Urubú phonology. ms.

Loewen, Jacob. 1968. Why minority languages persist or die. Practical anthropology 15:8-15.

Métraux, Alfred. 1950. A religião dos Tupinambás e suas relacões com a das demais tribus Tupí-Guaranís, Série 5, Brasiliana 267. Companhia Editora Nacional.

Montoya, Antonio Ruiz de. 1879. Conquista espiritual hecha por los religiosos de la compania de Jesus en las provincias del Paraguay, Parana, Uruguay y Tape. Rio de Janeiro.

Nida, Eugene A. 1954. Customs and cultures. New York: Harper and Brothers.

Ribeiro, Darcy e Berta G. Ribeiro. 1957. Arte plumária dos Indios Kaapor. Rio de Janeiro: Offset-Gráfica Seikel, S.A.

Service, Elman R. 1962. Primitive social organization. New York: Random House.

Spindler, George D. (ed) 1974. Education and cultural process toward an anthropology of education. New York: Holt, Rinehart and Winston, Inc.

Thevet, André. 1575. La cosmographie universelle D'André Thevet. Paris: Pierre l'Huilier.

www.ingramcontent.com/pod-product-compliance
Lightning Source LLC
Chambersburg PA
CBHW050539270326
41926CB00015B/3306